CHILDHOOD POVERTY AND SOCIAL EXCLUSION

From a child's perspective

Tess Ridge

First published in Great Britain in October 2002 by

The Policy Press
34 Tyndall's Park Road
Bristol BS8 1PY
UK

Tel +44 (0)117 954 6800
Fax +44 (0)117 973 7308
e-mail tpp@bristol.ac.uk
www.policypress.org.uk

British Library Cataloguing in Publication Data

A catalogue record for this book is available from the British Library

ISBN 1 86134 362 0 paperback

A hardcover version of this book is also available

Tess Ridge is a Research Fellow in the Department of Social and Policy Sciences at the University of Bath, UK.

Cover design by Qube Design Associates, Bristol.
Front cover: photograph supplied by kind permission of www.third-avenue.co.uk
Printed and bound in Great Britain by Hobbs the Printers Ltd, Southampton.

Contents

List of tables and figures

Tables

Acknowledgements

There are many people who have helped and encouraged me during this study, and my thanks go to all of them. My particular thanks go to all the children and young people who took part in this research. Their generosity in granting me an insight into their lives, and their openness and frankness during the interviews was deeply appreciated and I hope I have been able to stay true to their views and meanings and do justice to their accounts.

I would also like to thank the Economic and Social Research Council for their generous financial assistance (Fellowship Award No R000271232) and the Department of Social Security (now the Department for Work and Pensions) who were kind enough to draw a sample of children from their Income Support records. The data from the British Household Panel Youth Survey used in Chapter Six were made available through the Data Archive. The data were originally collected by the ESRC Research Centre on Micro-Social Change at the University of Essex. Neither the original collectors of the data nor the Archive bear any responsibility for the analyses or interpretations presented here.

I would also particularly like to express my gratitude and appreciation for the enduring encouragement and support that I have received from Professor Jane Millar of the University of Bath; as always her knowledge and insight have been invaluable. My thanks also to Jim Davis of The Children's Society for his inspiration and encouragement. Finally my deepest thanks for the love and support of Ember, Adam and Tom.

ONE

The challenge of child poverty: developing a child-centred approach

This book is about the lives and experiences of children in poverty; it provides an opportunity to understand some of the issues and realities of child poverty from a child-centred perspective. With 3.9 million children (nearly a third of all children in Britain) living in poverty[1] in 2000/01 (DWP, 2002a), the likelihood of spending part of their childhood in poverty has become a disturbing reality for many of Britain's children. It is therefore imperative that we have an informed understanding of how the experience of poverty and social exclusion affects children in their social and familial lives. We know from previous studies (Bradshaw, 1990; Kumar, 1993; Gregg et al, 1999; Bradshaw, 2001a) that growing up in poverty has severely adverse outcomes for many children. What we know far less about is how the experience of poverty and social exclusion impacts on children's own perceptions of their lives. We also have little understanding of how children interpret their experiences of poverty and how those experiences may be mediated through their differences and embedded in a diversity of social and structural environments. This book attempts to answer some of these questions by placing children at the centre of the inquiry and exploring the economic and social pressures that poverty brings to their everyday lives. This 'child-centred' approach underpins the process of research and analysis used throughout. At the heart of the book lie findings from a new empirical study of children and young people who are living in poverty (Ridge, 2000), which explores through their own accounts the economic, social and relational impact of childhood poverty and social exclusion. The book comes at a particularly opportune moment as policy makers and practitioners seek to address the economic and social disadvantages of childhood poverty and social exclusion, while endeavouring to move towards a more inclusive and cohesive society (DSS, 1999a).

The challenge of childhood poverty

> I will set out our historic aim, that ours is the first generation to end child poverty forever, and it will take a generation. It is a 20-year mission but I believe it can be done. (Blair, 1999, p 7)

Blair's historic pledge in 1999 to end child poverty within 20 years meant that the issue of childhood poverty moved, at last, from the periphery to the centre of the policy agenda. This is a welcome development and in stark contrast to the preceding 20 years, when childhood poverty was marginalised or denied, even though the numbers of children in poverty showed a three-fold rise, from 1.4 million in 1979 to 4.5 million in 1998/99 (DSS, 1996, 2000a). Throughout that 20-year period, this extraordinary increase in child poverty remained largely unacknowledged in either political discourse or public policy (Bradshaw, 1990; Oppenheim and Harker, 1996; Walker and Walker, 1997). Therefore, the Labour government's public commitment to eradicating childhood poverty signalled a new and overdue interest in the lives and well-being of Britain's poorest children. To achieve its aim of eradicating child poverty in 20 years and of halving it in the next decade the government has embarked on a programme of radical welfare reform, which is intended to fundamentally change the systems of support for children in the UK. However, despite the much needed and welcome increase in policy attention and additional resources, ensuring that the needs and concerns of low-income children themselves are acknowledged and addressed presents a significant challenge for policy makers and professionals working with children.

Historically, children in poverty have remained largely absent from poverty discourse and public policy responses. Although policy is increasingly family-focused (Home Office, 1999), it is not necessarily child-centred, and children's interests and needs are easily subsumed and hidden within family interests and needs (Ridge and Millar, 2000; Ruxton, 2001). Anti-poverty measures directed towards children and their families have always been constrained by tensions between the interests of the state and the rights and responsibilities of the parent; in this arena the needs and rights of the child can come a poor third. Yet children are particularly vulnerable to changes in family policies, especially social security policy and the provision and adequacy of benefits. Even in today's policy climate, children have tended to appear in the policy process in complex ways: as burdens on their parents, as adults-to-be, as threats to social order and stability (Ridge and Millar, 2000). They rarely appear simply as children, with their own concerns, their own voices and their own agency.

Government has responded to child poverty in ways that have tended to focus on the futures of children who experience poverty in childhood, a concern for the child as the adult-to-be (DSS, 1999a; HM Treasury, 1999). This echoes traditional concerns about children that focus less on the lived experience of childhood and more on the child as an investment for the future, and this in turn leads to policies taking a particular form. However, the effects of poverty in children's lives need to be understood in both the short term (outcomes in childhood itself) and the long term (outcomes in adulthood) (Millar and Ridge, 2001). An important facet of that process must be an acknowledgement and understanding of the issues that concern children. Without an informed awareness of the economic and social pressures that disadvantaged children experience in the immediacy of their everyday lives, policies directed towards the alleviation of child poverty and social exclusion run the risk of failing to respond adequately to those children's needs.

What do we know about children in poverty?

Although historically childhood poverty has frequently tended to be ignored or obscured (see Chapter Two), there is now a considerable body of statistical knowledge which explores the dynamics and consequences of child poverty using data from a range of social surveys, including the National Child Development Study (NCDS) and the British Household Panel Survey (BHPS). These provide a comprehensive overview of the dynamics of child poverty, including durations and the extent and nature of persistent poverty in the UK (see Hill and Jenkins, 1999; and Jenkins et al, 2001, among others). Concern about the number of children living in poverty has meant that the measurement and monitoring of the economic well-being of children has greatly improved (see DSS, 1999a; Bradshaw, 2001b). We know an increasing amount about the degree to which children are experiencing poverty, and under what circumstances. Research indicates that children are vulnerable to high rates of poverty, and are likely to experience it over long durations and for repeated spells (Hill and Jenkins, 1999). There are strong links with worklessness, ethnicity, lone parenthood, sickness, disability, and long-term reliance on inadequate means-tested benefits (Bradshaw, 1990; Kumar, 1993; Oppenheim and Harker, 1996; Adelman and Bradshaw, 1998; Gordon et al, 2000; Howard et al, 2001; see also Chapter Two). These and other studies have also provided insights into some of the outcomes of poverty for children, including poor health, poor cognitive development, low self-esteem, poor educational achievement, homelessness, poor housing conditions, and poor environments (Bradshaw, 1990; Kumar, 1993; Hobcraft, 1998; Gregg et al, 1999; Machin, 1999; Bradshaw, 2001a; Ermisch et al, 2001).

Undoubtedly, these studies provide a valuable insight into the possible consequences for children of experiencing poverty in their childhood. However, much of the focus of quantitative studies has been on the impact of childhood poverty on the future adult; a greater understanding of the impact of childhood poverty in childhood itself may be obtained through child-centred research.

Can quantitative data be child-centred?

Accessing data suitable for a child-centred exploration of children's social lives is problematic. There is an almost complete dearth of statistical data that places children at the centre of analysis (Jensen and Saporiti, 1992), and children have tended to be ignored or excluded from social and statistical accounting (Qvortrup, 1997). Where children have appeared it is often as an adjunct to adult data, or in data concerned with the impact of children on adult lives and family economies. Interest in children's lives per se is still relatively rare (Scott et al, 1995). Large-scale surveys that focus on social and material enquiries at the individual and household level have all tended to exclude respondents below the age of 16 years. Increasing acknowledgement that children are not merely passive members of households but have their own views, attitudes and experiences to relate has gone some way towards increasing research with children and young people (see Middleton et al, 1994; Shropshire and Middleton, 1999).

Shropshire and Middleton (1999), using a children's questionnaire, raised concerns about the extent to which children's economic learning, behaviour and aspirations are affected by disadvantage. They found that children in poorer families may be 'learning to be poor', controlling their expectations and reducing their aspirations, in the face of their family's severely constrained economic circumstances. Some insight into why they may be reducing their aspirations and expectations may be gauged from surveys measuring childhood deprivation, using an index of socially perceived necessities. These reveal how deprived children are missing out on a broad range of essential items and activities enjoyed by their peers (Middleton et al, 1997; Gordon et al, 2000). The *Poverty and Social Exclusion* survey of Britain (PSE) shows that one third (34%) of British children go without at least one item or activity deemed as necessary by the majority of the population, and nearly one fifth (18%) go without two or more items or activities (Gordon et al, 2000). Studies such as the *Small Fortunes* survey (Middleton et al, 1997) and the *Poverty and Social Exclusion* survey of Britain (Gordon et al, 2000) establish through research with adults (mainly mothers) a list of items and activities that are considered basic necessities for children in Britain today. However, valuable as these are, they all entail adult perceptions of children's needs; there has been little engagement with children themselves about things that they themselves would consider essential for their material and social well-being.

Qualitative research with children

A greater insight into the lives of children living in poverty could be gained from qualitative research, which is inherently more reflexive and responsive. However, when moving from the more quantifiable aspects of childhood poverty to the social and relational impact of poverty and social exclusion in childhood, it is evident that there are considerable gaps in our knowledge. Despite the considerable body of statistical data relating to child poverty, there is a dearth of meaningful qualitative data. Indeed, it is only recently that adults in poverty have had any voice in poverty research, an area traditionally dominated by 'experts' (see Bradshaw and Holmes, 1989; Cohen et al, 1992; Kempson, 1996; Beresford et al, 1999). Although organisations such as the Child Poverty Action Group would appear to have a specifically child-focused perspective, to date little of their research has focused primarily on children themselves. Previous publications such as *Hardship Britain* (Cohen et al, 1992), while giving a rare qualitative insight into the experiences of people in poverty, have had no input from children. *Hard times* (Kempson et al, 1994) provides a valuable account of strategies used by families on a low income to meet their needs. However, although the study explored in detail the lives and experiences of 74 'families', children's voices and experiences in general were absent. *Life on a low income*

(Kempson, 1996) is a review of 31 qualitative studies in which people in poverty speak for themselves. Of the 31 studies chosen, however, very few provide an arena for children's and young people's voices to be heard (see Middleton et al, 1994; Anderson and Quilgars, 1995; Jones, 1995; Roaf and Lloyd, 1995). Of these, only *Family fortunes* (Middleton et al, 1994) involved interviews with children rather than with young people who had left their family homes. When children and young people leave the family home and enter the public domain either as 'victims' through homelessness and the care system, or as 'villains' through juvenile crime, they become more visible. Although a relatively recent phenomenon, studies which interview young homeless people, children in care or young care leavers, for example (Butler and Williamson, 1994; Biehal et al, 1995), are at last becoming more common and are an important aid to policy and developing an understanding of young people's lives and experiences. However, in general, as Bradshaw (1990) argued, we know very little about what children themselves think and feel about poverty; and 10 years on we are still in a similar situation.

For some qualitative understanding of the experience of poverty for children and young people, we must turn in the main to three publications, *Family fortunes* (Middleton et al, 1994), and two studies by the Children's Society, *Same scenery, different lifestyle* (Davis and Ridge, 1997), and *Worth more than this* (Roker, 1998). *Family fortunes* explores the economic pressures on parents and children in the UK. Children's involvement in the research was through group discussions and questionnaires, which explored their social lives and aspirations. The sample of children, aged 8-16 years, was drawn from schools and made up of children from diverse socioeconomic backgrounds, so in this case the focus was not primarily on children in poverty. Their responses were divided into two socioeconomic groups for analysis: the 'more affluent' and the 'less affluent'. The interviews explored with children how they spent their time, what possessions they had and what they felt they needed in order to participate in the world around them. They also explored the social pressures that children experience from peers. What emerges is a disturbing picture of how children from low-income families "begin to experience the reality of their 'differentness' at an early age" (Middleton et al, 1994, p 150). These issues are further highlighted by Davis and Ridge (1997) and Roker (1998) in two studies which explored the experiences of children and young people from low-income families from a child-centred perspective. What was particularly apparent using this approach were the social and peer pressures exerted on children; the financial demands of participation and the fears and social costs of exclusion.

What is currently missing in child poverty research?

Developing a more child-centred approach to understanding the experience of poverty and social exclusion in childhood will entail a radical rethink about the conceptual frameworks with which poverty has been traditionally analysed and understood. Much of our analysis of poverty has been framed within an adult discourse of economic distribution and material resources. If we broaden our perspective to include the more relationally dynamic notion of social exclusion, we are still no further enlightened. Although the notion of social exclusion is now an important part of mainstream political rhetoric, it is a poorly understood concept. Our ability to recognise the causes and consequences of social exclusion and our capacity for understanding and acknowledging the processes of social exclusion are still developing. It is also a concept that is open to different social, political and cultural interpretations and bias (see Levitas, 1998). Yet, whatever the values underpinning the different notions of social exclusion, the defining characteristics have always been predominantly adult centric.

Current political rhetoric and policy is directed towards a notion of social exclusion that is primarily concerned with exclusion from the labour market, and although many children are economically active, this approach is focused on adult experiences and needs and has little to tell us of the experience of social exclusion within childhood. When the dangers of social exclusion for children and young people do appear on the policy agenda, it invariably focuses on the child as the 'adult-to-be'. The prioritising of truancy, school exclusions, teenage pregnancies, homelessness and the 'worst estates' by the Social Exclusion Unit (see SEU, 1998a, 1998b, 1998c, 1999), while acknowledging some of the most serious problems facing society at present, also reflects adult concerns of 'youth' as a threat to social order and stability. Alternatively, children have been seen mainly as a future resource, as a form of human capital, to be protected and developed. Yet, while the effects of poverty and social exclusion will undoubtedly reverberate from childhood into adulthood, children experience social exclusion within the immediacy of childhood, among their peers. Therefore, social exclusion for children could signify much more than exclusion from society as conceived by adults. It may also mean exclusion from the norms and customs of children's society. In this respect, childhood needs to be seen as a social experience in itself, where the demands of participation and inclusion may be considerable, and likewise the costs of exclusion (Ridge and Millar, 2000).

Clearly, it will be hard to operationalise a concept of social exclusion relevant to children which is based on adult themes, because children are structurally and institutionally excluded from many of these areas at the outset. Therefore, any conceptual framework must be contextualised within the state of childhood itself. It would need to encompass the discourse, agency and identity of the child, while also recognising the stratifications of power inherent in adult/child social relations; and the social boundaries, constructions and institutions, which shape the experience of being a child.

What is child-centred research?

What does it mean to put the child at the centre of research and analysis? Much previous research involving children has been largely *on* them, rather than *with* them or *for* them (Hood et al, 1996). In the past, the main areas of interest have been the family, health and education. However, in all these fields, children's own perspectives have historically seldom been the central focus. Only recently through initiatives from the Economic and Social Research Council (ESRC)[2] and the Joseph Rowntree Foundation have children been seen as 'social actors' with their own stories to tell. Much research with children has been observational and heavily informed by the developmental paradigm, which confines children to a series of stages towards adulthood (Hood et al, 1996). This poses mature adulthood as the ultimate goal by which children are measured. The consequence of this is to confine children's lives and experiences to an adult agenda, where the effects of early childhood, educational achievement and so on have been studied for their impact on the adult-to-be rather than on the child of the present. This tendency is clearly evident in many studies of childhood poverty. Dominant assumptions about the nature of children and childhood have led to a model of the child as a 'research object' (Hogan and Gilligan, 1998). However, there is a growing recognition that children are social actors in their own right, rather than inadequately socialised future adults (James and Prout, 1997). This means a shift from 'object' to 'subject', and a recognition that children themselves are best informed about their lives and the issues that are meaningful to them. Children have their own set of opinions and judgements, which, while not always the same as those of adults, nevertheless have the same moral legitimacy (Fine and Sandstrom, 1988).

The assumption that children are 'naturally' incompetent and incapable is very socially pervasive and has often resulted in children being viewed as unreliable witnesses about their own lives (Qvortrup, 1994). As a consequence, adult proxies have often been used to speak for children. However, the use of adult proxies – parents, teachers, social workers and so on – raises issues of the reliability and veracity of such accounts. Adults' views of children and children's views of themselves may differ greatly (see Mahon et al, 1996), and issues perceived by adults as relevant to children might not be those articulated by the child (Ennew and Morrow, 1994).

Putting it into practice

Child-centred research practice requires an informed and considered approach at every stage of the research process. This means developing skill and sensitivity not just in the practical methodological techniques of establishing rapport, openness and trust (Butler and Williamson, 1994; Alderson, 1995), but also in acknowledging and addressing ethical considerations and issues of power and control (Morrow and Richards, 1996). Issues of access arise, and the need to ensure that informed consent is sought from children as well as the adults with their care; this is challenging in an environment where adults have the power to refuse consent even when children wish to participate (Thomas and O'Kane, 1998). Parents, teachers and other key adults in children's lives can equally assume children's consent, and the researcher needs to be particularly vigilant to ensure that children and young people are fully involved in the consent process. It can also be particularly hard for children to withdraw from, or discontinue, an arrangement made by key adults who have power in their lives (Hill et al, 1996). Space and privacy for children to talk in confidence will also need to be negotiated (Mauthner, 1997). Children are vulnerable, not only through their inherent weakness and dependence on adults, but also critically through their lack of rights and their lack of political and economic power. This is often overlooked, resulting in an overemphasis on children's physical vulnerability and a lack of focus on their structural vulnerability (Lansdown, 1994). However, although research must be informed by an awareness of children's vulnerability and dependence, it also needs to ensure that they are accorded respect and autonomy within the research process. Only by engaging directly with the child and seeing them as independent actors negotiating a complex social world, with an intricate web of social and familial relationships and loyalties, can a valid account be obtained.

Understanding children's experiences of poverty

The fundamental aim of this book is to develop an understanding of child poverty that places children at the centre of the analysis at all times. To do this, the book is organised into three sections, and uses a variety of different techniques to explore child poverty. The first section (Chapter Two) provides an historical and contemporary overview of childhood poverty. It traces how our understanding and knowledge of child poverty has grown and changed during the 20th century, and it examines historical representations of children in poverty. It also focuses on the current state of child poverty in the UK, and takes a critical child-focused look at the policies implemented by the Labour government in response to their pledge to eradicate child poverty in 20 years. The second section of the book (Chapters Three, Four and Five) is based on findings from a new qualitative study of children and young people living in families in receipt of Income Support. Also included in this section are findings from interviews conducted with a sample of parents, which explored their perceptions of issues that were highlighted by their children. The final section (Chapter Six) presents findings from a new quantitative study of children's experiences and perceptions of school, using British Household Panel Youth Survey (BHPYS) data. A description of the two main data sources used in the second and third sections follows.

The qualitative study

This was a new empirical study using in-depth interviews to explore the lives and experiences of a group of children and young people from low-income families. The fieldwork was carried out in the spring and summer of 1999, in urban areas of Bristol and Bath, and rural areas of Somerset. The children interviewed were drawn from a random sample provided by the Department of Social Security (now the Department for Work and Pensions). They were all living in families in receipt of Income Support, and had been so for more than six months. The sample was divided into lone-parent and two-parent families. Two-parent families were families where an adult or a child was disabled, rather than using the more usual characteristic of unemployment. This enabled a better match between lone-parent families and two-parent families, as both types were likely to experience poverty over a long duration[3]. Children were also grouped according to their location and the sample was divided between rural and urban children. This enabled a comparative exploration of potentially differing experiences. Children and their families were approached on a random basis, within the parameters of family type and location, and interviews were carried out until the required sample size of 40 children was attained.

The final sample of 40 children and young people contained 20 children from each family type, 10 each from rural and urban locations. There were 19 girls interviewed and 21 boys. Ages ranged from 10 to 17[4], with the majority of the sample aged between 10 and 15 years (34), and over half of the sample (22) between 10 and 12 years. All children and young people in the sample were white, which reflects the make up of rural areas for the 20 children in the rural sample. The urban sample was approached on a random basis using inner-city postcodes. However, no families in ethnic minorities were encountered before the sample of 20 children was completed. Wherever children in families had siblings who were within the age category these were also interviewed.

Poverty is in many ways a socially unacceptable word, heavily imbued with stigma and prejudice. Therefore, research which seeks to explore the nature and impact of poverty needs to be conducted with great sensitivity. This is especially so when the research subjects are children and the research agenda requires considerable openness, trust and self-reflection. Previous research with children using a group environment has proved very fruitful (see Burgess, 1984; Middleton et al, 1994; Hill et al, 1996). However, logistically there are few opportunities to get children together, other than in an institutional setting such as a school, where there are inherent difficulties in selecting out children who are from low-income families from others, without reinforcing stigma. Therefore, the study used individual in-depth interviews which made it easier to ensure confidentiality and privacy. It also provided a safer and more intimate environment for disclosure and exploration of sensitive issues such as friendship and self-esteem, issues which could be obscured or leave a child painfully exposed in the shared environment of a group interview.

The interviews explored children's experiences at school, at home and with their families; and it focused on their economic and material environment, their social relationships and their own understandings of the impact poverty has made on their lives. Because the interviews were designed to be as child-centred as possible, a very flexible and unstructured interview procedure was chosen, which evolved over the fieldwork period, incorporating new areas of interest as they were identified by children. Children are rarely seen as individuals in their own right, and generally subsumed into the family. By interviewing siblings within families it is possible to gain some understanding of how children within families may experience their circumstances very differently.

All the interviews were taped and subsequently transcribed. Analysis of the data was carried out manually using thematic indexing. Themes included those issues initially highlighted in the interview schedule and were broadened out to include issues identified by children themselves. The interviews had been structured in a few areas, for example whether or not children received any pocket money; this allowed some basic comparative work to develop some generalisations and identify differences. A comparative approach was also adopted to identify any key differences between children on the grounds of gender, age, family type, and location (rural or urban). Differences between children and young people who were or were not working were also examined and where siblings had been interviewed, their responses as individuals and as family group members were noted and explored. All children's names have been changed to anonymise the data, and care has been taken at all stages to ensure the primacy of children speaking for themselves.

In addition to interviews with children and young people, interviews were also conducted with 17 parents of the children in the sample. This was a smaller sample and was not intended to mirror the child sample. Interviews with parents were only undertaken when parents were uncertain about the interview process, and wished to be reassured about the process, or when they particularly wanted to have their say about bringing up children on a low income. However, as most parents were happy for their children to be interviewed, the opportunity was taken to interview the child, and where appropriate their siblings, rather than to request an interview with the parent/ s. Of the interviews conducted with parents, nine were lone parents and eight were parents from two-parent families. The parents were interviewed separately at the same visit as their children, and all interviews, with children and parents, were completely confidential; each was unaware of any comments the others may have made. All interviews were taped and transcribed. The interviews and analysis focused on adult perceptions of areas already highlighted by children. This ensured that as far as possible it was the children's issues and concerns which set the agenda.

The quantitative study

The quantitative study analysed a cross-section of data from the BHPYS. This is a survey that utilises child-centred research ethics, and is a unique and important source of data relating to children's leisure activities, health, and their attitudes to family, education and work. However, despite its potential, this is a rarely used data set, and previous analysis has tended to focus on children's health and mental well-being (see Brynin and Scott, 1996; Brynin, 1997; Clarke et al, 1999; for a recent exception see Ermisch et al, 2001). Because of the child-centred nature of the collection and generation of the data, and its coverage of social relationships and social attitudes, this was a uniquely suitable data set for the purposes of this study (see the Appendix for an overview of the BHPYS data).

The data was used to explore how children and young people experience their school environment. This is one of the most critical areas in children's lives. Current education policy is increasingly driven by demands to improve academic standards. But school also plays a particularly significant role in children's lives as a site of social as well as pedagogical learning. There is also increasing interest in the school as an environment for developing 'soft skills'[5] for future employability. The greater parts of children's social interactions with other children are also contextualised within the school environment. Analysis of the BHPYS data provided an ideal opportunity to explore children's and young people's experiences and perceptions of school life and their relationships with their teachers. Wave 7 (1997 data), the latest issue of data at the time of analysis, was used to explore children's experiences, and analysis was carried out on a cross-sectional sample of 720 children and young people who were aged between 11-15 years. The data compared the responses of children living in families receiving Income Support and/or Jobseeker's Allowance with those of children who were in families that were not receiving these benefits.

Understanding the everyday challenges of a childhood in poverty

Throughout the book, the decision was made to focus on children's everyday lives and experiences. Many of the issues that have traditionally been associated with the lives of children in poverty – on the one hand, drugs, drinking, prostitution, school exclusions and truanting, and on the other, violence, neglect and abuse – are of critical concern. But there is also a need to understand and acknowledge some of the other everyday experiences and demands that the majority of children from low-income families face. Normative perceptions of 'poor' children's lives have often been informed through media-induced panics, and stereotypical images that focus mainly on child abuse and neglect, or drug abuse and criminality (Scraton, 1997). The images engendered are of 'poor' children as either villains or victims (Daniel and Ivatts, 1998). Negative stereotypes obscure the everyday realities of such children's lives and impinge on their rights to social justice. These one-dimensional images not only shape and distort social perceptions and understandings of children in poverty, they can also affect the lives of disadvantaged children among their peers, fostering stigma and the potential for difference and exclusion. One of the underpinning aims of this book is to redress the balance somewhat, to facilitate an awareness of child poverty that can incorporate a richer and far more complex understanding than our present perceptions allow, of the everyday challenges faced by children who are 'poor'.

Notes

[1] Defined as 60% of median income after housing costs.

[2] The ESRC 5-16 Research Programme consists of 22 linked research projects looking at different aspects of children's lives in contemporary society.

[3] Children in two-parent families in receipt of sickness and disability benefits are more likely to experience a longer duration of means-tested benefit receipt than those in two-parent, unemployed families (DWP, 2002b).

[4] The few 17-year-olds included were still living at home and attending school, therefore classified by the DSS (now the DWP) as child dependants.

[5] Employers in the UK are increasingly stressing the importance of 'soft skills'. These are poorly defined at present but include personal qualities, friendliness, teamwork, communication skills, the ability to fit in and so on (Sparkes, 1999).

TWO

What do we know about childhood poverty?

To develop a child-centred understanding of childhood poverty it is necessary to have some insight into how children in poverty have been represented and treated over time. This chapter is concerned with exploring representations and perceptions of child poverty and it begins with a brief historical overview, tracing how our understanding and knowledge of childhood poverty has grown and changed during the last century. In doing so it examines historical and contemporary representations of children in poverty from a child-centred perspective and takes a comparative look at the UK in relation to the European Union and the rest of the 'developed' world. The chapter continues with an exploration of the current situation of children from low-income families in the UK, and identifies some of the key risk factors that affect children's vulnerability to experiencing episodes of poverty. It also takes a critical child-centred look at the current policy responses to childhood poverty and their implications for children's lives.

An historical overview of childhood poverty in the UK

Throughout history, children have rarely featured in contemporary accounts; representations of childhood as a lived experience are remarkably absent. In particular, the voices of children living in poverty have rarely been heard. As Laslett (1971) points out, in the pre-industrial world there were children everywhere, and yet "these crowds and crowds of children are strangely absent from the written record" (1971, p 110). As we move towards the 20th century our perceptions and understandings of children and childhood are informed largely by paintings, poetry and fiction; idyllicised accounts of particular representations of childhood. The autobiographical accounts that survive are largely reflexive and involve adult memories of past childhoods, rather than any contemporaneous accounts of childhood and the experiences of poverty. Due to the growing tradition of working class and feminist oral history, many voices are now being heard that would otherwise have previously been lost. These accounts have given us a rich and valuable insight into the world of the child, particularly through life in the late 19th and early 20th centuries (see Thompson, 1981; Vincent, 1981; Burnett, 1982; Davin, 1996). Yet autobiographies are never completely representative of the whole society, and the poorest classes are the least represented (Burnett, 1982). Consequently, the voices and experiences of children in poverty have been doubly obscured, both as children and as part of the population of 'the poor'.

Clearly early representations of child poverty have in most cases come from neither children nor the poor; however, what representations we have "constituted the frames within which the details of state and philanthropic action were formulated" (Cunningham, 1991, p 233). Any historical account of the lives and experiences of 'poor' children needs to be embedded in a wider account of the social, economic and political developments over time. We start our overview with a look at the Poor Law, where the treatment of children reveals some of the deep ambiguities that persist in some of our perceptions of 'poor children'. Are children a representation, and extension, of their parents, locked into and already 'corrupt' with the 'taint' of their parents' poverty? Or are children in need of succour and assistance in their own right? These are issues that are still socially active today, albeit often under the guise of media-induced moral panics (see Goldson, 1997).

The Poor Law

During the 19th century, the most obvious sign of poverty was recourse to the Poor Law where two main systems of relief existed: the workhouse and Outdoor Relief. In the 1834 Poor Law Amendment Act, the Poor Law Commission assumed that children would be dealt with in the same way as their parents, therefore the principle that 'children should follow their parents' was adopted (Pinchbeck and Hewitt, 1973). Consequently, children of the 'able-bodied' poor had to follow their parents into the workhouse. Given the rigours of the workhouse, principles of 'less eligibility' and the moral approbation and stigma attached to pauperism, it is evident that recourse to the Poor Law must have been an act of extreme desperation for families in need. Therefore, the numbers of children in poverty and destitution was likely to be far higher than statistics compiled by the Poor Law Commissioners suggest. By 1838 the numbers of children in the workhouse had risen to 42,767, representing half of all those in the workhouse population (Pinchbeck and Hewitt, 1973). In response to this growing population, administrators of the new Poor Law were forced to modify their treatment of children. Changing perceptions of poor children, allied with concerns about endemic pauperism, surfaced in the *Fourth Report by the Poor Law Commissioners* (1838).

> The pauper children Maintained in Union workhouses are dependent not as a consequence of their errors, but of their misfortunes. They have not necessarily contracted any of the taint of pauperism. They are orphans or deserted children, or bastards, or children of idiots, or of cripples, or of felons, or they are resident in the workhouse with their parents, who seek a brief refuge there. (Kay, 1838, Appendix, p 140)

The report reinforced the importance of education as "a means of eradicating the germs of pauperism from the rising generation" (Kay, 1838, p 140). The recommendations concerned separating children from adults in the workhouse and the provision of a basic education.

However, reformist measures such as educational provision were largely directed at children within the workhouse; there was little or no educational provision for the much greater numbers of children on Outdoor Relief (Duke, cited in Fraser, 1976). These children, although numerically far greater than those in the workhouse, were the least visible, and as a consequence were treated very differently. There was considerable indifference towards these children, who were assumed to be under the care of their families. They were classed not as individuals in their own right, but merely as 'dependants' of the destitute person (Webb and Webb, 1929a). It was not until 1873 that Parliament required that Boards of Guardians should in all cases make it a condition of Outdoor Relief that children aged between 5 and 13 should be in regular attendance in public elementary school; 35 years after such measures were introduced for workhouse children (Webb and Webb, 1929b). This lack of interest and concern illustrates how the 'familialisation' of children and childhood, the phenomenon whereby children are "thought of as belonging to the family – to the extent that they in many contexts disappear as individuals" (Qvortrup, 1994, p 22), can obscure the realities of children's lives.

Much of the public discourse of childhood poverty at this time concerned the issue of children at work, in mills, mines and factories; and there was a new and growing preoccupation with the importance of childhood and children's right to protection (Cunningham, 1991). These preoccupations generated a new type of philanthropist, concerned about the quality of children's childhoods, and influenced by a new ideology of childhood (Cunningham, 1995). Among the philanthropic endeavours that sprung up at the time were the religious voluntary childcare societies such as the Church of England's Waifs and Strays Society and Dr Barnado's. The religious motivation driving the societies meant that the overriding concerns were with 'rescuing' children and 'saving' them from parental and environmental depravity. Fundamental to this mission was the removal of children from their 'corrupt' parents[1].

Many societies saw themselves as having full parental rights over children when they were in their care and discouraged any contact between parents and children. Once in control, societies felt justified in dealing with the children as they thought fit; in effect this resulted in a policy of child emigration to the colonies[2]. Ward (1998) argues that the practices of voluntary societies established grounds and laid the foundations for legislation transferring parental rights and responsibilities to a third party. Poverty was the underpinning factor which precipitated the decision to separate children from their families and Ward asserts that although material circumstances have improved, poverty is still a defining factor in children's admission into the public care system today (see Bebbington and Miles, 1989[3]).

The 1880s saw the beginning of a shift in balance between philanthropy and the state and state action began to take over from philanthropic endeavour on behalf of the child. There was a growing involvement of professionals, and experts became concerned with the task of 'saving' children (Cunningham, 1995). There was a range of motivations underpinning the concern for children and much state action was driven by concerns for population levels, and the quality of citizens, especially for the future of the state and the empire. These concerns were also reflected in the growing tension between the state and the family around the needs of the child and the rights and responsibilities of the parents. The social fears of the 'poor' child, as the potentially dangerous adult-to-be, highlight the ongoing tension between notions of 'deserving' and 'undeserving poor', and the difficulties associated with childhood poverty are clearly exposed.

Childhood poverty at the beginning of the 20th century

While the extent of poverty throughout the 19th century had been a matter of contentious public debate (Scott, 1994), the beginning of the 20th century saw the emergence of attempts to develop a more scientific and systematic approach to the measurement and understanding of poverty. The science of studying and categorising 'the poor' led to a greater awareness of poverty and an increasing understanding that certain groups were at greater risk of experiencing poverty than others; with this came a gradual realisation that children made up a significant proportion of the poor. However, children were rarely, if ever, the focus of poverty studies and their disproportionate vulnerability to poverty often emerged only as an adjunct to the study of adult poverty. In effect, children were more likely to be highlighted as a cause of adult poverty, than to be recognised as a group that was itself highly vulnerable to poverty.

The earliest scientific attempts at researching and measuring the extent of poverty began with the sociological work of Charles Booth in the 17 volumes *Life and labour of the people in London* (1902-03). Throughout Booth's first series, *Poverty*, the extreme conditions of childhood poverty and immiseration are revealed. His commentary on the conditions of children expressed the concerns of the age; children were "the raw material out of which to a great extent the poverty, misery and vice of the next generation are being evolved" (Booth, 1902-03, p 232). Booth was clear that children needed to be fed, by their parents, charity or the state, as a portion of their natural rights. However, he also expressed fears that provisions such as free school meals would remove from the "shiftless and indifferent" the "natural and wholesome stimulus" to provide for their families. His concerns reflected the current mood of the time and the tensions between a concern to relieve hunger and need in children, the desire for minimal interference in families, and the value attached to parental responsibility.

Close on the heels of Booth's study of London came Seebohm Rowntree's study of poverty in the city of York in 1899 (1901). Rowntree found that 7,230 people were affected by 'primary poverty[4]'; however, he was not drawn to comment on the fact that 4,215 (58%) of these were children. The poorest children largely form a silent backdrop to Rowntree's early work, and his exploration of family poverty invariably focuses on the adults in the family. This lack of focus and interest in children is revealed in the fieldwork notes where the particulars of children are recorded in the investigators' notebooks under the remarks column, along with the condition of the house and so on, for example, "Five children under nine. Untidy, overcrowded" (1901, p 51).

Despite his tendency to overlook the significant number of children in poverty, Rowntree highlights the inner dynamics of families being in poverty who are constantly living from hand to mouth.

> Extraordinary expenditure, such as the purchase of a piece of furniture is met by reducing the sum spent on food. As a rule in such cases it is the wife and sometimes the children who have to forgo a portion of their food; the importance of maintaining the strength of the wage-earner is recognised, and he obtains his ordinary share. (1901, p 83)

Strategies to survive hardship within families were essential, however, as Vincent (1991) points out; within the family the experience of hardship differed sharply according to age and gender. "Deprivation did not standardise suffering, nor did it break down long established divisions of responsibility and power" (Vincent 1991, p 6).

Rowntree also made a considerable contribution to the understanding of poverty by identifying a 'poverty cycle', five alternating periods of want and plenty in a labourer's life[5]. In doing so he highlighted childhood as a period when the child would probably be in poverty, followed by a period of comparative plenty when living with parents but earning; then follows a period of want when he himself has young children to support. As his children become earners they contribute to the family and a period of plenty is regained, only to be lost again during old age. Rowntree's cycle of poverty drew attention to the importance of children as determinants of adult poverty, not only as a drain on resources, but also as workers and contributors. However, his main direct contribution to the understanding of childhood poverty was his examination of the physical condition of school children[6], and the highlighting of their poor physical condition and malnutrition. His findings had an important impact on the growing concerns about the needs of the state and the empire. In the ensuing debate, much attention was directed towards the health and well-being of the nation's children. In the early part of the 20th century the tensions between the state and the family over the welfare of children intensified.

Children as future citizens

Concerns about national fitness had surfaced during the Boer War (1899-1902), where three out of every five soldiers were deemed unfit to enlist (*BMJ*, 25 July 1903, cited in Gilbert, 1966). At this time, despite the tensions between the state and family responsibility, there was sufficient policy pressure to move towards welfare provision for children, such as school medical inspections and the 1906 Education (Provision of Meals) Act, which compelled local authorities to provide school meals for children deemed in need. However, these were seen as educational measures, intended to ensure that children were in a position to benefit from their schooling, rather than as anti-poverty measures (MacNicol, 1980).

MacNicol (1980) argues that the concept of national health that emerged in the early 20th century was only meaningful in terms of military and industrial efficiency. By the inter-war years, when "militaristic fervour had waned and a vast army of unemployed provided a pool of surplus labour, there was less immediate concern over the health of future generations" (MacNicol 1980, p 44). During the inter-war years, there was considerable research into poverty and nutrition (for example, Bowley and Hogg, 1925; Tout, 1938). The evidence that children were disproportionately suffering from poverty was growing. However, despite the evidence of poverty and malnutrition in large families, and pressure from groups such as the Children's Minimum Council and the Family Endowment Society (Rathbone, 1924), there was a steadfast denial by the government of the need to raise the economic status of women and children (MacNicol, 1980).

In 1936, Rowntree conducted a further survey of York (Rowntree, 1941), in which – unlike his initial survey – children were individually recorded and the seriousness of their conditions recognised and highlighted. The disproportionate number of children suffering from the direst poverty was apparent and inescapable and Rowntree went on to make a strong plea for the provision of a minimum wage and Family Allowances. Rowntree's findings revealed children's vulnerability to poverty, especially due to factors of unemployment, low pay, large family size and living in female-headed households (lone-parent families created as a result of widowhood). His findings coming in the mid-1940s were an important factor in gathering momentum towards the 1945 Family Allowances Act (MacNicol, 1980).

After the 'welfare state'

The 1940s saw the birth of the British 'welfare state', and hopes were high that full employment, National Insurance and other redistributive fiscal and social policies would be instrumental in eradicating poverty. Childhood poverty was going to be a thing of the past which had no place in the new welfare state of the future.

It was not until the 1960s that there was a revival of interest in poverty, with the publication of Abel-Smith and Townsend's (1965) *The poor and the poorest*. Using secondary analysis of Family Expenditure Surveys, their findings indicated that a significant number of children and their families were experiencing poverty; clearly childhood poverty had not gone away. Indeed, as Vincent (1991) points out, there had always been a substantial number of children maintained on National Assistance or living in families that were below the National Assistance level (NAB Reports, 1955, 1964). Beveridge's system was unable to cope with economic and demographic change. The Family Allowance introduced in 1945 (but uprated only twice between 1948 and 1967), was inadequate and increasingly incapable of keeping low-income families out of poverty (Vincent, 1991).

The publication of *The poor and the poorest* was to act as a catalyst in the 'rediscovery' of child poverty, and Abel-Smith and Townsend were instrumental in the emergence of a new pressure group for the poor, the Child Poverty Action Group (CPAG) (McCarthy, 1986). Despite the name, CPAG did not focus exclusively on child poverty, although it did have a strong agenda to publicise family poverty and to act as a poverty pressure group on government. However, as McCarthy points out, there were considerable difficulties in forcing family poverty onto the political agenda (McCarthy, 1986). As Wynn (1968), a strong advocate of family policies has argued, children belong to the 'silent classes', with no effective representation of their economic and political interests.

In the late 1960s and 1970s, inroads were made in reducing the level of post-war poverty and inequality. Child welfare, and particularly concern about child poverty and an acceptance about the desirability of reducing inequalities between men and women, characterised much of the policy debate (Walker and Walker, 1997; Kiernan et al, 1998). While there had always been a minority of children in families suffering from poverty due to low wages, unemployment, and increasingly lone parenthood, real improvements in living standards, in health and welfare, meant that the overall situation of children had improved (Halsey, 1988; Bradshaw, 1990). However, the election in 1979 of the Thatcher administration heralded a new policy era, driven by free market economic policies where inequalities were not seen as damaging to the social fabric (Walker and Walker, 1997).

Childhood poverty from the 1980s onwards

This period is characterised by dramatic increases in poverty and income inequality as the Conservative government pursued what Walker (1990) has called a 'strategy of inequality'. The outcome for children in the 1980s and early 1990s was a devastating increase in childhood poverty and deprivation. Concerns about the well-being of children in industrialised societies prompted the United Nations Children's Fund (UNICEF) to commission a national study of child poverty and deprivation in the UK. The report by Bradshaw (1990) found that during the 1980s post-war trends towards greater equality had halted and been reversed. The number of children living in poverty had doubled; and it was children who had borne the brunt of changes in the economic conditions, demographic structure and social policies of the time.

The 1980s were characterised by a massive increase in inequality. The Joseph Rowntree Foundation's *Inquiry into income and wealth* (Hills, 1995) found that one of the most striking features was the relative concentration of children in the bottom of the income distribution. "They are 30 per cent of the poorest tenth, but only 13 per cent of the richest" (Hills, 1995, p 11). In the period from 1979 to 1992/93 children were the group most vulnerable to poverty in society as a whole. In 1992/93 there were 4.3 million children living in poverty compared to 1.4 million in 1979[7] (Oppenheim and Harker, 1996).

Kumar (1993) charts the trend in child poverty and the impact of widening income and wealth inequalities on children in the UK in the 1980s. He revealed an appalling catalogue of increasing material and social deprivation as escalating unemployment, low pay and a growing group of lone parents with poor economic prospects took its toll on children's lives. Homelessness, family breakdown, increasing ill-health and morbidity and poor educational outcomes provide a desperate picture of children profoundly affected by the rise in childhood poverty. The 1980s signalled a return for children of the spectres that had dominated Rowntree's early studies: vulnerability to poverty from unemployment and lone parenthood. Children in families with no full-time employment substantially increased their representation in lower-income groups. In 1979, 20% of children lived in families without a full-time worker; this had risen to 36% by 1993/94 (DSS, 1996). Where children in Rowntree's 1901 study were intensely vulnerable to poverty in a female-headed household caused by widowhood, they were now vulnerable to the effects of demographic change, and to increases in families headed by unmarried, divorced and separated mothers.

The gendered nature of poverty revealed in Rowntree's survey was again reproduced; lone-parent households are mainly headed by women, and are highly vulnerable to benefit dependency and poverty (Millar, 1989). In 1980 there were 320,000 families headed by lone mothers receiving Supplementary Benefit; by 1993 this had risen over three-fold to 989,000 receiving Income Support[8] (DHSS, 1981; DSS, 1994). In the political climate of the 1980s, policies were formulated that were not concerned with family poverty or gendered inequalities, but rather with establishing responsibilities for children between parents, in ways that reduced the cost of children and in particular the cost of lone-mother families to the state and therefore 'the taxpayer' (policies such as the 1991 Child Support Act) (Kiernan et al, 1998). The 1980s had led to very different lifestyles and outcomes for children.

> The lives of children in a two parent, two-earner family, living in owner occupied housing, in the south of England, served by good public services have improved. In contrast the lives of children in an unemployed or lone parent family, living in rented accommodation, in the inner city with deteriorating health, education and social services have got worse. (Bradshaw, 1990, pp 51/52)

Child poverty at the beginning of the 21st century

At the end of the 20th century children in Britain were some of the poorest in Europe and the 'developed' world. Data from the European Community Household Panel (ECHP) reveals the comparative situation of child poverty in the UK and the rest of the European Union in the early 1990s. Table 2.1 shows the proportion of households below the poverty line[9] in 1994 as 17% in the EU 12 as a whole, with Denmark having the lowest percentage at 9% and the UK having one of the higher percentages of households in poverty, at 23%. The proportion of individuals living in poverty in the EU 12 as a whole was also 17% and again the UK had one of the highest percentages of individuals in poverty at 22%. However, it is when the proportion of children living in poverty are examined that the dire situation of children in the UK compared to the rest of Europe is truly revealed. Denmark (5%), France (12%) and Germany (13%) have comparatively low percentages of low-income children aged under 16. While the UK, with one third of children aged under 16 in poverty (32%), has the highest rate of child poverty in the EU compared to one fifth of all children in the EU 12 as a whole (20%) (Eurostat, 1997).

Comparisons of indicators of child well-being which encompass more than just an economic poverty measure have a similarly poor showing for the UK compared with other countries in the EU (Micklewright and Stewart, 2000a). The UK's performance is worse than the EU average for five out of the seven child-specific economic and social indicators. On three of them, child poverty, worklessness and teenage birth rate, the UK's performance is the worst in the EU (Micklewright and Stewart, 2000a). Micklewright and Stewart argue that while in some areas the UK is better, or at least no worse than other EU countries, "the overall picture provides much cause for concern, with the UK emerging as a serious contender for the title of the worst place in Europe to be a child" (Micklewright and Stewart, 2000a, p 23).

While the UK can be seen to have a very high childhood poverty rate compared with other countries in the EU, a comparative look at the position of UK children in relation to the rest of the 'developed' world in the 1990s exposes an equally grim picture. Table 2.2 is based on Luxembourg Income Study data[10]. It shows the UK childhood poverty rates in relation to 24 other countries in the 'developed' world. In a table ranking countries according to the severity of their childhood poverty rates, the UK was ranked third worst, just behind Russia and the US (Bradbury and Jäntti, 2001). The UK had also seen one of the fastest accelerations in the childhood poverty rate[11], yet, this is in an environment in which many countries have been able to stabilise or even decrease their child poverty rates[12].

The European Observatory on National Family Policies has pointed to a complex mix of demographic factors that have had an influence on the UK's performance in respect of child poverty. These include comparatively high rates of fertility, young first-time marriages, divorce, and the resulting high proportion of lone parents; plus a high proportion of larger families with three

Table 2.1: Percentage of poor households, individuals living in poor households, and children living in poor households in the European Union (ECHP) (1994)

Country	Households	All individuals	Children under 16
Belgium	13	13	15
Denmark	9	6	5
Germany	13	11	13
Greece	24	22	19
Spain	19	20	25
France	16	14	12
Ireland	21	21	28
Italy	18	20	24
Luxembourg	14	15	23
Netherlands	14	13	16
Portugal	29	26	27
UK	23	22	32
EU	17	17	20

Source: Eurostat (1997); ECHP, first wave (1994)

or more children (Ditch et al, 1998). Jenkins et al (2001), comparing child poverty rates in the UK with Germany in the 1990s, found that differences in poverty rates between the two countries were explained only in part by poverty-triggering events, such as parental unemployment and family breakdown. Of greater significance was the superior performance of the German welfare state in protecting children and their families from the negative effects of these events. Therefore, while demographic characteristics are important, much will depend in each country on issues of labour supply and earnings, and the tax and benefit packages that countries provide to support parents with the costs of raising children (Bradshaw and Barnes, 1999). As Bradshaw (1999) argues, "child poverty is not inevitable – countries make more or less explicit choices about how far they employ social and fiscal policies to mitigate the impact of pre-transfer forces" (1999, p 396).

Current child poverty in the UK

Children who are poor are often viewed as an undifferentiated whole, an homogeneous group. Yet children's lives are diverse, and their risks and experiences of poverty will differ. Without a richer and more comprehensive view of the variety of children's lives and their experiences of poverty, we may miss factors that protect and strengthen children's lives, as well as those which may undermine them. Gender, age, ethnicity, class and employment status, family structure, sibling size (that is, the number of brothers and sisters children have), ill-health and disability are just some of the factors that can shape and

Table 2.2: Relative child poverty rates across the 'developed' world, showing percentage rate below 50% of median income

Country	Year	50% of overall median income	Rank
Russia	1995	26.6	1
US	1994	26.3	2
UK	1995	21.3	3
Italy	1995	21.2	4
Australia	1994	17.1	5
Canada	1994	16.0	6
Ireland	1987	14.8	7
Israel	1992	14.7	8
Poland	1992	14.2	9
Spain	1990	13.1	10
Germany	1994	11.6	11
Hungary	1994	11.5	12
France	1989	9.8	13
Netherlands	1991	8.4	14
Switzerland	1982	6.3	15
Taiwan	1995	6.3	16
Luxembourg	1994	6.3	17
Belgium	1992	6.1	18
Denmark	1992	5.9	19
Austria	1987	5.6	20
Norway	1995	4.5	21
Sweden	1992	3.7	22
Finland	1991	3.4	23
Slovakia	1992	2.2	24
Czech Republic	1992	1.8	25

Source: Bradbury and Jäntti (2001)

mediate children's lives and experiences. We know that there are several key factors that serve to make children particularly vulnerable to experiencing poverty. These include: living in a lone-parent family, living in an ethnic minority household; living in a large family; living in a family where there is an adult or a child with long-term sickness and disability; and living in either a workless household or one dependent on low pay (Bradshaw, 1990; Kumar, 1993; Oppenheim and Harker, 1996; Adelman and Bradshaw, 1998; Gordon et al, 2000; Howard et al, 2001). Looking at each of these factors in turn it is apparent that these are not discrete risks but elements of disadvantage that can intersect and reinforce each other.

Approximately three million children live in lone-parent families and they are particularly at risk of experiencing poverty during their childhood (Rowlingson and McKay, 2002). These children are disproportionately likely to experience life reliant on the lowest levels of means-tested benefits, and life on benefits may also mean experiencing poverty for a long duration; in 2002 over a third (34%) of lone-parent claimants had been receiving Income Support for more than five years (DWP, 2002c). The majority of lone parents are women and the risk of low income in these families is a reflection of gender inequalities within marriage and within the labour market (Millar, 1989). Children in lone-mother households have higher rates of poverty than children in couple families and tend to stay poor for longer (Bradbury et al, 2001). The number of children living in lone-parent families is also steadily increasing, leading to larger-sized lone-parent families, and a greater number of children affected by policies directed towards lone parents (Haskey, 1998). Living in a lone-parent household should not inevitably lead to poverty. Access to work and childcare, or in the absence of work, adequate provision of social transfers, will all have an impact on whether lone parents and their children suffer from poverty and disadvantage (Christopher et al, 2001). For example, Norway and Sweden have high rates of children in lone-parent families but low rates of child poverty, even though lone-parent families are still worse off than other family types in these countries (Bradbury and Jäntti, 1999). Studies such as Gregg et al (1999) have found that where there is no financial hardship in lone-parent families there is no evidence to link growing up in a lone-parent family with childhood disadvantage.

Research focusing specifically on ethnic minority children is very scarce. However, studies such as Adelman and Bradshaw's (1998) analysis of the Family Resources Survey indicate that Pakistani and Bangladeshi children in particular suffer extraordinarily high poverty rates, with around 80% of children living below 50% of median income poverty line after housing costs. Census analysis using Sample of Anonymised Records (SARs) to create an index of deprivation for children found that black Caribbean and Pakistani children were three times as likely to be suffering severe deprivation than white children, and Bangladeshi children five times as likely (Moore, 2000). Platt (2000), analysing Housing Benefit data, suggests that a higher proportion of children from minority groups are living in poverty and that the severity of their poverty is greater than that of white UK children, although white UK children are more likely to experience poverty continuously.

For children in minority ethnic groups racial discrimination plays a major role in their likelihood of experiencing poverty. Data from the Family Resources Survey for 1995/96 shows that while ethnic minority groups make up only 6% of the population, they make up 11% of the poorest fifth (Hills, 1998). Inequalities in the labour market leave ethnic minority groups vulnerable to low pay and unemployment; the risk of unemployment for people from ethnic minorities is nearly three or four times higher than that of white people (Howard et al, 2001). A younger age profile also means that families from ethnic minority groups are particularly vulnerable to changes in family policies, such as frozen rates of Child Benefit and so on.

Sibling size is also an important factor in children's likelihood of experiencing poverty. The *Small Fortunes* survey found that children with two or more siblings were more likely to be poor than 'only' children or those with one sibling (Middleton et al, 1997). Latest data from the Households Below Average Income Statistics (HBAI) shows that 'only' children are the least likely to be in the bottom quintile of the income distribution, whereas 4 in 10 children in families with three or more children were in the bottom quintile, and almost 7 in 10 were in the bottom two quintiles (DWP, 2001). Large family size is also a factor for some ethnic minority groups, especially for Pakistani and Bangladeshi families. The Fourth National Survey of Ethnic Minorities (Modood et al, 1997) found that 33% of Pakistani families and 42% of Bangladeshi families had four or more children.

The links between poverty and disability are well established (see Thompson et al, 1990; Berthoud et al, 1993). Households with a disabled child are among some of the 'poorest of the poor' (Gordon and Heslop, 1999). Families with more than one disabled child are likely to be lone parents, workless, in low-paid employment, or reliant on Income Support (Lawton, 1998). There are also children living in families where there are adults with disabilities and long-term sickness. Children in these families not only share their family's experiences and durations of poverty, but may themselves have the added responsibilities of caring at a young age (Becker et al, 1998). These are some of the least visible of low-income children, and they are likely to experience long durations of poverty that are comparable to those experienced by lone-parent families. In 2002, 76% of children in families where there was sickness and/or disability were receiving a key benefit (either Incapacity Benefit, Severe Disablement Allowance, or Income Support with Disability Premium) for two or more years (DWP, 2002b). Disability within a family and the attendant reliance on means-tested benefits over a long duration can also lead to anxiety and debt (Grant, 2000).

The employment status of the household in which children live has also been shown to present a major risk of poverty for children. In 1995/96, 54% of all children in poverty (over 2.3. million children) were living in workless households (Gregg et al, 1999). The UK also had the highest rate of children in workless households across the EU, with 19.5% of households with children under 15 years living in households where there was no adult worker, compared with an EU average of 10.6% (Micklewright and Stewart, 2000b). Worklessness impacts on many different family types, in particular there are large numbers of lone-parent families where there is no working adult (Bradshaw, 1999), and worklessness is high among certain ethnic minority households. Families where there is a parent who is sick or disabled will also suffer a high degree of worklessness. The rise in workless households has occurred within the context of increasing polarities of work status, reflected in a simultaneous rise in the number of dual-earner households and in the number of workless households (Gregg and Wadsworth, 1996). This has led to even greater disparities between 'work rich' and 'work poor' households.

The impact of worklessness on children's lives gives rise to concern, not only for the economic disadvantages it brings, but also for the potential for stress and tension within the family and the dangers of limiting children's aspirations and social contacts (Micklewright and Stewart, 2000b). However, like lone parenthood, unemployment need not necessarily mean poverty for families. Again, the level of social transfers, in this case unemployment compensation, can act to mitigate the circumstances of unemployed families. A study by Papadopoulos (2000) has shown that short-term unemployment assistance in the UK is comparatively low for the EU, and in the UK unemployed people are very dependent on means-tested benefits. In addition, although worklessness is clearly a major factor in child poverty, the presence of an adult worker does not automatically mitigate those circumstances; changes in the labour market and rising numbers of insecure jobs, part-time earnings and low wages have all contributed to many children experiencing poverty within working households. In 1995/96 nearly 700,000 children lived in poor households with only part-time or low-paid earnings (Gregg et al, 1999).

Along with concerns about the depth and severity of child poverty, the lengths of time children spend in poverty are also important for developing an understanding of the short- and long-term effects of children's disadvantage (Gregg et al, 1999). A study by Hill and Jenkins (1999) identified two types of child poverty: 'chronic' and 'transitory' poverty[13]. Their analysis of panel data from the BHPS (1991-96) provides a six-year longitudinal perspective on child poverty. They found that both chronic and transitory poverty were of a 'sizeable magnitude' among British children, especially among the very young. They argued that although reducing transitory poverty is important, reductions in chronic poverty deserve more attention. Clearly many poor families move in and out of poverty, however, some, such as lone-parent families, experience extended periods of disadvantage. As Walker (1995) points out, "repeated spells of poverty in a life lived close to the margins of poverty, or recurrent spells of severe and long lasting hardship" (1995, p 127) may each require very different policy responses. Nevertheless, although the focus on chronic poverty is essential, transitory spells of poverty during childhood can also be particularly damaging. Given the nature of childhood as a period of intense social, emotional and physical development, what might be considered as a short period of time in an adult's life can encompass periods of significant growth and development in a child's life.

What is apparent from an exploration of these different risk factors in children's lives is that they are interlocking and in many instances reinforcing. Children living in lone-parent households are also likely to be living in workless households. Children in Pakistani and Bangladeshi households are likely to have parents receiving low wages and will possibly have several siblings, and so on. Clearly, children's lives are very diverse. Children in poverty will live in families whose circumstances will ebb and flow, reflecting not only their material resources, but also the social and cultural conditions prevalent in our society. It is evident that policies to end child poverty must respond to these risk factors, and address the environment and circumstances in which children in poverty are living. Many of the risk factors identified above have an enduring quality, being strong indicators of poverty for children at the beginning, as well as the end of, the 20th century. However, in the first part of this chapter we saw how tensions between the state and the family constrained policies to directly address child poverty throughout the last century. When child poverty was forced onto the public agenda, the response was often underpinned by moral or political concerns that addressed the needs of the state rather than the needs of the child. In this final section we shall look at the current Labour government's response to spiralling child poverty rates at the start of the 21st century, and explore the implications for disadvantaged children of Labour's pledge to end child poverty within 20 years.

Labour and child poverty

The election of the Labour government in 1997 signalled a major change in the policy agenda. Labour had inherited one of the poorest records of child poverty in the developed world (Bradbury and Jäntti, 1999). However, initially there was no specific manifesto commitment from Labour to reduce child poverty (Millar and Ridge, 2002), and during their first year of office there was little sign that the government considered it a pressing issue. Indeed, one of their first acts in government was to remove the lone-parent premium, delivering a severe blow to the incomes of some lone-parents and their children[14]. However, in 1999, Tony Blair announced that his government was committed to eradicating child poverty within 20 years. This was later followed by further commitments to half it in 10 years and, in a Public Service Agreement, to reduce it by at least a quarter, by 2004 (DSS, 2000c). This has meant a considerable flurry of policy activity, resulting in a major programme of welfare reform directed at reducing child poverty. This covers a wide range of policies and falls into three broad areas:

- support for children, mainly through the education system;
- support for parents, mainly directed at making work pay, childcare and parenting initiatives;
- changes in fiscal support for children and families via the tax and benefit system.

To monitor the outcomes of its anti-poverty policies, Labour committed itself to annual poverty audit reports under the title *Opportunity for all*, which have set out specific and measurable indicators relating to the well-being of children (DSS, 1999a, see below).

This is a welcome development and is in stark contrast to the preceding 20 years. Measures to support children include targets for improved literacy and numeracy skills, action to reduce truancy, school exclusions and teenage pregnancies, and broader investment in Education Action Zones[15]. There is also the provision of Sure Start initiatives in England and Wales, and Family

Centres in Scotland. The initial aim was for 250 local programmes by 2002, reaching almost 20% of disadvantaged children under four (Brown, 2000). These are targeted at the most vulnerable pre-school children and their parents, and funding has been increased over time; it was doubled in the 2000 Treasury Spending Review (HM Treasury, 2000a). For older children, Education Maintenance Allowances (EMAs) will be introduced for low-income children who wish to stay on in education after the school leaving age. They provide up to £30 (£40 in a few areas) to help young people with their studies. Originally piloted in 15 areas, EMAs will be rolled out nationally in September 2004. ConneXions, a new support service for young people which began full-scale operation in 12 areas from April 2001, offers a range of guidance and support for 13- to 19-year-olds, to help with the transition to adult life. The Children's Fund, with a budget of £450 million over three years, is mainly targeted at preventive work with children in the 5 to 13 age group. The Fund will be rolled out across the whole of England by 2003-04. Children's Fund partnerships are expected to provide services such as mentoring, after school clubs and parenting support.

A fundamental tenet of the government's strategies to reduce child poverty is the importance of a proactive welfare system, designed to get people into paid work (DSS, 1999a). To this end, welfare reforms are directed towards encouraging workless adults, including lone parents, into the workplace through the New Deal initiatives; and at ensuring that work will pay, through the introduction of the minimum wage and a reformed in-work benefits system which replaced Family Credit with a tax credit, Working Families' Tax Credit (see below). Underpinning these measures is a major investment (initially £470 million) in a National Childcare Strategy to ensure that childcare is available for all parents who wish to work. Coupled with this is an increase in the number of pre-school nursery places, with guaranteed places for all 4-year-olds and 66% of 3-year-olds by 2001/02 (DSS, 1999a). Alongside these measures are a whole tranche of policies designed to improve skills and human capital and to encourage family friendly employment practices. Outside of policies directed towards work, there are also measures to tackle adult literacy and to improve parenting skills, particularly among the most vulnerable children and their families, through the Sure Start programme.

In line with the government's stated aim of making work pay, a radical overhaul of the in-work benefits system has resulted in a shift in administration of some benefits from the Department of Social Security (now called the Department for Work and Pensions) to the Inland Revenue. Family Credit (FC) has been replaced by the Working Families' Tax Credit (WFTC), which is now administered by the Inland Revenue, and this has meant that families receive their 'in-work benefit' in the form of a tax credit usually in the wage packet. WFTC is targeted at low-income working families but also specifically at encouraging women such as lone parents into the workforce. Paid at a higher rate than FC, and with a longer taper, there is also a Childcare Tax Credit to offset the costs of childcare. The government asserts that these more generous allowances, coupled with a disregard of child maintenance when WFTC is calculated, mean a guarantee that lone parents working for 20 hours or more, with young children, will be above the poverty line even when rent is paid (Brown, 2000). There is also a new Children's Tax Credit, which replaced the Married Couples Allowance, and it is worth £20 per family per week for standard rate taxpayers.

For those children living in families receiving Income Support there has also been an improvement in premium rates for children aged under 11. The staged increase has consolidated the premiums into one rate. In 1997, the premium for under-11s was £16.90 per week, and for up to 16-year-olds £24.75. Increases in successive budgets have resulted in a substantial increase, leading to a current payment of £32.95 for all children aged under 16. Increases in Income Support rates for younger children amount to an 80% rise in real terms between 1997 and 2001 (Lister, 2001). This is a considerable improvement in the incomes of households with children and is particularly intended to address the previous inadequate level of Income Support premium allowed for young children, which had been highlighted by Middleton et al (1997).

Child Benefit has also been increased in real terms, by 27% for the first child and 3% for subsequent children (Piachaud and Sutherland, 2001). Current levels are £15.75 for the first child and £10.55 for second and subsequent children. Child support is also undergoing reform, and parents who are primary carers will now be allowed to keep up to £10 per week more of their Income Support benefits when they receive maintenance payments, and these will be fully disregarded for claimants of WFTC (DSS, 1999b).

Following close on the heels of these benefit changes is the intention to provide a single system of support for children by means of the Child Tax Credit in 2003. The intention is to provide a 'seamless system' of support, which ensures a secure income to help the transition between welfare and work, and will be paid regardless of parental work status. This will entail rolling up child components of Jobseeker's Allowance/Income Support with the Children's Tax Credit and the child components of WFTC to create a single system of support. Millar (2000) argues that this is a potentially important element in the drive to reduce child poverty. It should improve work incentives, ease the transition into work, improve social inclusion by treating all families alike, and as it is being paid to the main carer it will ensure that the money goes straight into the family budget. It is also an important acknowledgement of society's obligation to ensure secure and continued support for children. Announcing the new tax credit, Treasury Minister Dawn Primarolo heralded it as a "new streamlined system [which] will provide a secure stream of income for children, whether parents are in and out of work, helping people make the move into work and removing stigma from support for children" (Primarolo, 2001).

Alongside these reforms have come tentative signs of a new approach to children and young people. Labour has made some progress towards more involvement of children themselves in policy developments. There has been a series of consultations with children and young people across the country, including the Policy Action Team 12 report on young people, and the setting up of a Children and Young People's Unit (with a brief to administer the Children's Fund). These are important, although still limited, steps towards a more 'child-centred' approach to policy making and policy evaluation. Overall, children and young people have become much more visible in the policy process, and this is itself a significant development (Millar and Ridge, 2002).

Implications for children of current policies

It is clear from the welfare reforms discussed above that this is a period of intense policy activity. These are very valuable and important welfare changes, and the centrality of child poverty to the policy agenda after years of marginalisation is to be welcomed. Evidently, the impact of these policy reforms on the number of children experiencing poverty could be considerable. Many of the issues highlighted earlier in this chapter are being addressed, including support to leave benefits and to enter paid employment, through the New Deal programme, increased investment in childcare, and the availability of in-work childcare allowances. The provision of higher rates of in-work benefits to supplement low earnings will also go some way towards addressing the needs of the working poor. The needs of very young children are acknowledged through the early intervention of Sure Start programmes, and increases in Income Support premiums and Child Benefit. Measures to improve numeracy and literacy and increased investment in education are also vital components of addressing disadvantage. However, there are caveats, and while no one would deprecate the laudable aim of eradicating child poverty, there are critics of some aspects of the reforms. These include the extensions of means testing, and concerns about the emphasis on paid employment and the absence of support for full-time parental care (see Hirsch, 1999; Lister et al, 1999; Piachaud and Sutherland, 2000).

My focus in this study, however, is not on the overall content of the reforms, but in developing a child-centred understanding of childhood poverty and social exclusion. To this end it is important to ask what the implications of these reforms for children themselves are and whether the government is truly addressing the needs of poor children. We have seen at the beginning of this chapter how policies directed towards the family have often served the needs of adults and in particular the needs of the state above the needs of children. Children cannot be separated from their families, but each reform will have an impact, intended or unintended, on children's lives.

First, given the historic tensions between the state and the family, it is apparent that the state decided to shift the public/private divide and involve itself extensively in areas that were previously considered the realm of the family. Thus, the emphasis on parental literacy and the provision of Sure Start to provide parenting classes, and advise on nutrition and so on, and the conditions attached to mothers on Income Support receiving the maternity grant[16]. These are all measures which are directed at tackling the problems of the youngest and most vulnerable of poor children, and directly involve the state in influencing and controlling parental behaviour. They are targeted at poor families and can easily carry the stigma of selection as a 'poor parent' in more than one sense. The success of programmes like Sure Start may well depend on ensuring that they attract a broader base of parents than those on Income Support, and are seen as a community resource rather than a service directed at the poor. Nevertheless, the importance of early years development has been acknowledged, and measures such as Sure Start will play a vital role in protecting children at the start of their lives.

Second, the main thrust of government policy has been directed towards returning people to the labour market. This has important implications for parents, especially for lone mothers, who are one of the main targets of the policies. For children there is little dispute that the increase in household income from a working parent is an advantage, and this is a key component in the government's strategy to lift children out of poverty, even though it is estimated that 7% of children in working families will still be below the poverty line (Piachaud and Sutherland, 2001). However, there is the potential for tension in this approach between the needs of the child and the needs of the adult and the state. For many children, increased involvement of their parent/s in paid employment may mean a much longer time away from home, travelling to childcare, or breakfast clubs, and staying on at after-school clubs or with childminders. Children, many as young as four years old, are already engaged in a school working week of approximately 30 hours. These are not necessarily disadvantages for children but they are factors that will impact on children and affect their lives. Given the implications for children of greater involvement in institutions external to the home, there must be some concern about the type and quality of childcare that children from low-income families will be able to access.

It is also apparent that even given the emphasis on paid employment, there are many children in families for whom paid work is not an option. It was estimated that about 800,000 children would be lifted out of poverty due to the 1998 and 1999 Budget measures (Piachaud and Sutherland, 2000). In addition, following the 2000 Budget, the Treasury estimated that between 1.2 and 1.9 million children would rise above the poverty line (HM Treasury 2000b). However, latest government poverty figures show that the government's anti-poverty strategies have not been as successful as anticipated, and child poverty has only fallen by 0.5 million, from 4.4 million in 1996/97 to 3.9 million in 2000/01 (Brewer et al, 2002). Reducing child poverty is proving difficult even for a government with a stated commitment to eradicating child poverty within 20 years. Furthermore, even if the government's strategies to promote paid work was an unqualified success, there are still expected to be over two million children in poverty (Piachaud and Sutherland, 2000).

Many of the children who are expected to benefit from welfare-to-work measures, tax and benefit reforms, will be living in families whose incomes are close to the poverty line. The remaining children will be in families that are much harder to reach. Many will be young children below the age of five and many will be in lone-parent families or families where there is sickness and disability. Of greatest concern, however, must be those children who are living in families that are still reliant on means-tested safety-net benefits such as Income Support. Despite the welcome increases in child premiums for children under the age of 11 years, there is still no overall increase in adult Income Support rates and these remain inadequate for the support and maintenance of families with children (Family Policy, 2000; Holman, 2000). Recent analysis by Bradshaw (2001) using a Low Cost but Acceptable (LCA) budget, shows that while recent increases in Income Support, especially for younger children, have narrowed the gap between the LCA and Income Support levels, there is still a gap of £5.95 per week for a lone parent (with two children aged under 11) and £11.17 per week for a couple family (with two children aged under 11). The LCA budget is also well below average living standards, and does not encompass the realities of life for families on Income Support, where Child Benefit is deducted, and budgets are often burdened by debt repayments.

A look at the measures intended directly to address children's social and developmental needs shows that these measures are directed mainly at the school environment, and focus almost entirely on academic issues related to numeracy and literacy, and reducing school exclusions and truancy. But there is little evidence for an association between school exclusions and poverty; and school exclusions affect only a small proportion of pupils. While these are important concerns for children, the degree of social inclusion that children experience at school and at home is also vital. Yet we have little knowledge or understanding at present about how poor children experience school and how poverty might affect children's relationships with their teachers and their peers. The government rhetoric of social exclusion has been primarily focused on adult worklessness, and the importance of welfare-to-work measures to address it. There has been less said and considerably less conceptual understanding or acknowledgement of the problems of social inclusion facing poor children themselves.

Finally, as a result increased of concern about child poverty there is now a considerable body of statistical data relating to many aspects of children's lives (for example, see Howarth et al, 1998; Bradshaw, 2000a; Ermisch et al, 2001). Nonetheless, there is still a long way to go before we have a comprehensive and insightful picture of childhood poverty. In particular, reliable data relating to many issues that affect children, including how many children are living in homeless families, rates of morbidity among children and poverty among children in minority ethnic groups, is still hard to find.

The government's child poverty indicators could be more comprehensive, and, in particular, they could include other measures which would give a greater awareness of disadvantaged children's lives. Bradshaw (2001a), using evidence from the ESRC research project 'Poverty: the outcomes for children', lists 17 extra outcome measures which are known to have an association with child poverty and which would be valuable additions; these included measures such as low birth weight, child death rates and children living in temporary accommodation. In addition to these he highlights other indicators that are not poverty outcomes but which could provide a valuable insight into the circumstances of poor children. They include the percentage of children living in families receiving Income Support/Income-related Jobseeker's Allowance, and the percentage of children living in households lacking three or more socially perceived necessities. These are important issues, and the indicators related to socially perceived necessities pose the question, how do we determine what children's socially defined needs are? So far, research has done so by talking to parents rather than to children themselves.

Summary

The situation of children in poverty has clearly changed over the last century. The severe poverty at the turn of the 20th century was replaced by a reduction during the middle part of the century, only to be followed by a catastrophic rise during the 1980s and early 1990s. What is most apparent from this brief overview of the history and representations of childhood poverty is the almost total absence of children's own voices, accounts and experiences. As subjects and citizens in their own right, children have remained largely absent from poverty discourse and public policy responses, and the experiences and needs of children in poverty have frequently been ignored or obscured. When child poverty is revealed it is either as an adjunct to adult poverty, or as an explanatory factor for adult poverty, rather than being seen as a serious issue in its own right. However, when the realities of childhood poverty have been inescapable and the issue has been forced onto the public agenda, policy responses have invariably been informed by an underpinning set of moral, religious or political issues, such as concerns for national and industrial efficiency evinced at the beginning of the 20th century. Public policy responses to child poverty have been almost overwhelmingly preoccupied with an interest in children as future citizens and workers, rather than as children negotiating a childhood marked by the experience of poverty and deprivation.

An exploration of some of the key factors that affect children's risks of experiencing poverty reveal how family structure, employment status, ethnicity and parental health are all influential. These are not discrete categories of risk but rather economic, social and cultural factors, which intersect and interact with the economic, social and political environment of their time. In this context, we explored the Labour government's response to child poverty and their commitment to end child poverty within 20 years. Their policy agenda involves a radical overhaul of the welfare system, and in particular of systems of support for children. These are important initiatives and entail a comprehensive 'joined-up' approach to tackling child poverty. However, the fundamental creed underpinning the government's strategy to reduce child poverty is the belief in the labour market as the primary agent of social inclusion.

Consequently, the main thrust of government policy is directed towards welfare-to-work and the privileging of paid work. This, as we have seen, raises questions about what impact these reforms will have on disadvantaged children, and whether their needs are foremost in the policy agenda. It has become apparent that even in the unlikely event that all of the government's welfare-to-work strategies succeed, without a significant element of redistribution and improved social transfers, there will remain a substantial number of children in poverty.

However, a particularly welcome and radical aspect of the current government's policies has been their intention to develop a greater understanding of children's lives and an increased involvement of children and young people in the policy process. The following chapters, based on children's accounts of their lives and experiences in poverty, are intended to go some way towards furthering that process. Through the development of an insight into child poverty that is grounded in a meaningful understanding of children's everyday lives, it becomes possible to envisage a response to child poverty that is, on the one hand, more complex and diverse, and on the other, more responsive to the needs and concerns identified by low-income children themselves.

Notes

[1] A study of the records of 400 children admitted to the Waifs and Strays Society between 1887-94 reveals that only a third of the children were so-called 'rescue' cases, while at least 46% were children admitted by their parents as a direct result of poverty (Ward, 1998).

[2] During the period between the late-Victorian and Edwardian years, more than 40,000 children were sent overseas to work as farm labourers and rural domestics (Hendrick, 1994).

[3] Bebbington and Miles' (1989) study of 2,500 children in local authority care in the 1980s identified six significant factors predating entry into care, five of which were known to be either causes or consequences of poverty, and the sixth the result of discrimination.

[4] "Families whose total earnings are insufficient to obtain the minimum necessaries for the maintenance of merely physical efficiency" (Rowntree, 1901, p XIX).

[5] Rowntree's focus is invariably on men and the lives and experiences of women would have been very different.

[6] Children were weighed and measured and their physical condition noted. Rowntree (1901) found that the poorest children were smaller and considerably underweight compared with other children. More than half of the poorest children were classified as in bad health, poorly fed and showing signs of neglect.

[7] Defined as 50% of average mean income after housing costs.

[8] Income Support replaced Supplementary Benefit in 1988.

[9] Eurostat define a poor household as those living below each country specific poverty line, defined as 50% of mean annual equivalised income in each country.

[10] A measure using 50% of median income.

[11] For the period 1985-95 there was an 8% increase in the child poverty rate in the UK (Oxley et al, 2001).

[12] For the same time period a number of countries which had high child poverty rates experienced a decline, in particular, Australia, Canada, Greece, Turkey and the US (Oxley et al, 2001).

[13] A child was defined as in 'chronic' poverty if they were below the poverty line for six years; if a child was poor some time during the six years but not chronically poor s/he was classified as experiencing transitory poverty (Hill and Jenkins, 1999).

[14] In April 1997 Family Premium and Lone Parent Premium were combined to form Family Premium (Lone Parent). From April 1998 Family Premium (Lone Parent) was abolished, although those already in receipt continued to receive it until their circumstances changed (DSS, 2000b).

[15] Education Action Zones involve local partnerships made up of schools, local education authorities, parents, businesses and the local community. They are charged with developing innovative approaches to raising school standards in disadvantaged areas.

[16] The Maternity Grant was increased from £100 to £200 in March 2000, followed by a further increase to £300 in Autumn 2000. Now called the new Sure Start Maternity Grant, to be entitled to receive it the mother, or her partner, must have received information about child healthcare from their doctor, midwife or health visitor.

THREE

Children's access to economic and material resources

The following three chapters present the empirical findings from in-depth interviews with 40 children and young people living in poverty. They cover three main areas in children's lives; this chapter explores the financial and material aspects of children's lives; Chapter Four looks at the social and relational aspects, focusing in particular on children's lives at school; and Chapter Five focuses on the children's home environment and their personal and familial lives. The paramount aim of the qualitative study was to use children's own subjective accounts to develop a child-centred understanding of childhood poverty and social exclusion; as a consequence, wherever possible children's own voices have been used to illustrate their accounts.

Material resources and capabilities

In this chapter, we focus on children's accounts of their opportunities to access economic and material resources, and explore some of the socioeconomic issues that children raise. Childhood, like adulthood, is deeply steeped in the consumer culture of our time. A higher standard of living leads to increasing demands and escalating pressures on families struggling to achieve adequate social integration and social standing. Childhood has its own social and cultural demands, and children's need for financial resources and their desire to attain certain commodities reflects not just the 'common culture of acquisition' (Middleton et al, 1994) but also the significance of consumer goods as a means of communication between young people (Willis et al, 1990). The children in this sample were living in families where they were likely to be experiencing poverty over a long duration. Thus, the issue of children's capacity to access adequate financial and material resources to ensure social participation was one that clearly had profound implications for them.

To explore the importance of economic resources in these children's lives, this chapter focuses on three key areas:

• Children's and young people's access to pocket money as a secure financial resource. Pocket money or an allowance is the main medium through which children and young people generally gain access to their own source of money. This first section explores whether children in low-income families were able to access their own reliable source of pocket money, and what role pocket money played in their lives.

- Children's and young people's engagement in employment. Paid work is a potential source of income for children, but the issue of child employment from an adult perspective is a complex one. However, the aim here was to understand the nature of work from a child's perspective and to gain some insight into the role work plays in the lives of low-income children. In this section, children talked about their experiences of work, and highlighted some of the issues that work raised for them in their lives.
- The importance of transport in children's and young people's lives and the role of transport as a key to social involvement. During the interviews, access to transport was identified by children themselves as a major issue in their lives. This final section looks at why transport was an important material resource for children and explores whether these children were able to gain sufficient access to affordable transport to ensure that they had the capacity to maintain adequate social functioning with their peers.

Throughout the chapter, children's own voices and accounts will be used to highlight the issues that are discussed, and their meanings and interpretations of the issues raised are of central concern. Parental interviews will also be used to provide an holistic and contextual insight into some of the issues that children have identified.

Pocket money: as a secure financial resource

Pocket money was an important issue for children, who have their own thoughts and feelings about its use and value. There has been considerable research interest in the development of socio-economic skills in children (Abramovitch et al, 1991; Feather, 1991; Lewis et al, 1995), yet there has been very little research conducted with children themselves which focuses on the meanings and values that they attach to pocket money[1]. Previous research has indicated that children's knowledge and understanding of money was directly related to their experiences of dealing with money, especially their opportunities to earn, save and spend money (Marshall and Magruder, 1960; Marshall, 1964; Abramovitch et al, 1991; Feather, 1991). In an increasingly complex economic world, the provision of pocket money or an allowance is one of the main agents through which children learn socioeconomic competency, and develop their capacities as economic actors. The importance of early economic socialisation has been recognised by the government and recent changes in the school curriculum mean that children are to be taught how to manage their pocket money, and to develop financial literacy (Carvel, 1999). However, there has been little research focusing on children living in households where income was already constrained. Children experience the realities of their economic world within their families, but they are also exposed to different economic realities in interactions with their peers and through their engagement with the wider world. For children in low-income families, where financial resources and material goods may be constrained, access to pocket money may play a very particular role in their lives.

Access to pocket money

The interviews explored with children whether they received any pocket money and what their experiences of pocket money had been. When asked whether they received any pocket money, only 12 of the 40 children said that they received pocket money on a regular basis. As Table 3.1 shows, eight children said that they received pocket money only rarely or irregularly when their parents could afford it, and 20 children responded that they did not receive any pocket money at all. Boys were more likely than girls to have irregular pocket money and girls were marginally more likely to have no pocket money than boys. There was no difference between family types.

The most striking finding was that over two thirds of the children (28 out of 40) were not receiving any pocket money, or were only receiving money on an irregular basis. Previous research with children indicates that in general, only a minority of children do not receive pocket money (Hill, 1992; Furnham 2001). However, poorer children are least likely to receive pocket money. Research by Lewis (2001) found that only a third (34%) of parents in social classes D and E[2] were giving their children pocket money compared with two thirds or more of parents in more affluent class groupings. Irregularity in pocket money payments are often a reflection of necessity and the need for families to maintain control over restricted resources. Shropshire and Middleton (1999) found that while 74% of 5- to 16-year-olds in the *Small Expectations* survey received pocket money, children in families in receipt of Income Support were three times as likely as other children to be given pocket money irregularly; furthermore, children in lone-parent families were twice as likely to receive pocket money irregularly compared with two-parent families. In general there has been little qualitative research which looks specifically at children in low-income families with regard to their access to financial resources, and the particularly high percentage found here may well reflect the severe financial constraints within these families, as well as children's perceptions of what pocket money is.

Table 3.1: Receipt of pocket money, by gender and family type

Receipt of pocket money	Yes	No	Irregularly	All
All	12	20	8	40
Girls	6	11	2	19
Boys	6	9	6	21
Lone-parent family	6	10	4	20
Two-parent family	6	10	4	20

Children and young people receiving regular pocket money

There were no substantial differences between gender or family types in the actual receipt of pocket money; six girls and six boys received pocket money, and six children from two-parent families and six from lone-parent families. However, not all pocket money came from parents and not all pocket money was provided unconditionally. Children were asked where their pocket money came from, and whether they were free to spend it as they chose. Most of the children received their pocket money mainly from their parents, although grandparents also played a significant role in providing extra resources for children in lone-parent families. For a few of these children, this was extra to their pocket money from their mothers, but for some of the others, it was the only source of money. While non-resident parents might be thought to play a role in the provision of pocket money for their children, no children reported receiving money regularly from their non-resident parents. Pocket money was not always freely given as a resource with no strings attached, and three children were doing chores in the home in return for pocket money from their parents. Studies of parental motivations for giving pocket money show that for younger children it was often used as a diffuser of tension between children's needs and demands and parental control of money and resources (Sonuga-Barke and Webley, 1993; Middleton et al, 1994; Lassarre, 1996). However, for older children pocket money and allowances are intended to educate and help young people develop consumer discernment and money management skills.

All of the children said that they received their money weekly; there were no children on monthly allowances, and some children reported that their money would 'go down' when their parents were particularly short of cash. Although there were considerable variations between the amounts that children received, ranging in general from £1-£5 per week, the most common amount was £1, less for younger children and more for older. There was one 13-year-old receiving £10 a week and one 16-year-old who was receiving only £1 a week, the same as most 10-year-olds.

Money for social life and possessions

Pocket money was used for a variety of things, although for most children it was a means to buy sweets and treats. However, some children were also clearly managing their money, saving it to buy clothes and other necessities including things for school, and using it for bus fares and social events with their friends:

> "Mostly we just buy sweets and sometimes if mum can't afford it we only get 50p or something." (Julie, 11 years, two-parent family)

"I save it up and I sort of like buy clothes and things with it, and other things I want." (Sue, 11 years, lone-parent family)

Of those children who were receiving regular pocket money, there was one child, the only lone child in the study, who was able to command a much greater amount of money than all the others. She received over £10 a week through drawing on a combination of sources. She explained how she got some from her mother and then more from other wider family members:

"I get a fiver a week, that does me because I am very careful with money, I save so that lasts me. My nan gives me money nearly every week as well so that's usually a fiver every week as well so that's a tenner every week. My aunt as well she usually does, I go up her house as well." (Colleen, 13 years, lone-parent family)

For children and young people who were receiving pocket money, it was evident that that even small amounts of money provided an opportunity for autonomy and some limited control over financial circumstances. Children without regular pocket money were in a very different situation.

Children without regular pocket money

Previous research has shown that children living in low-income families are less likely than others to receive regular pocket money, and this was often driven by necessity, especially for families on Income Support (Middleton et al, 1994; Shropshire and Middleton, 1999). However, research has shown that money received on an ad hoc basis was rarely satisfactory for children, and was often seen by them as not really pocket money at all (Hill, 1992). In this section, children receiving irregular amounts were considered together with those who received none, because the conditions under which they received their occasional odd payments were too irregular and too unreliable to count as pocket money. Therefore, their experiences of pocket money were similar in nature to those children who did not receive pocket money at all.

Several of the children said that they used to get pocket money but were now no longer receiving it. In many instances, a change in circumstances had brought about a loss of income, particularly in the event of parental illness and disability. For others, changes in family structure, the departure of a parent or step-parent or just severely straightened circumstances had brought about the change:

"I used to get a bit when my step-dad was living here but I don't no more." (Kevin, 12 years, lone-parent family)

"We used to but we've stopped that now. I don't know why we just stopped it." (Laura, 15 years, lone-parent family)

Two children who were not receiving any regular pocket money talked about occasionally getting some money from their non-resident fathers, although this was rare. Expectations of getting pocket money from non-resident parents was not very high, and several children appeared resigned to hoping for some money but never actually receiving it. In one girl's case, although she said she had been promised £5 pocket money a week from her father, it was not forthcoming and she had not received any for the last six weeks. However, once again grandparents often played an important role providing a valuable, if irregular, source of money for children who do not receive pocket money in general. By giving money on odd occasions, they appeared to ease some of the pressure between children and their parents, particularly when special events cropped up:

> "Sometimes like if I haven't got any money to go on a weekend, I won't ask my mum 'cos I don't want to ask her.... But I'd like to try and get some money somehow like. I dunno, 'cos like my nan might give me some money, a pound or something." (Laura, 15 years, lone-parent family)

Nicole lived in a large family where pocket money was rarely available. She relied very heavily on her grandparents for the chance of having any money to spend on herself. If she was lucky she received £1 a week, and she used this to go into town to see her friends:

> "Bus fares going into town, sometimes I save it and, like, try and, like, save enough money to get like a new pair of trousers and that takes me ages." (Nicole, 13 years, lone-parent family)

Negotiating strategies and alternative sources of income

Finding the money to be able to go out with friends and to engage in social activities was clearly important for children. Without pocket money, they were very reliant on their parents finding the money on an ad hoc basis. Children were essentially engaged in a complex set of monetary negotiations within their families. When they talked about how they tried to get money from their parents to go out, they revealed a subtle understanding of their parents' financial situations. This incorporated both an element of persistence in trying for money and an element of resignation in accepting that their parents were in many cases just unable to find the money for them:

> "I can remember saying to dad, 'Well could you just give me...'. 'Cos one of my friends got like 20p a day or something and by the time the end of the week come, because she hadn't spent it over the week she'd have like £2 or something to go swimming with or something.... So I said 'Can you do that?' but the thing was like it's 'Oh I haven't got the change today', and it's

just like.... So you forget really and you just don't bother." (Lisa, 15 years, two-parent family)

Another possible source of money for some children was in doing chores around the house, and some children said that they worked in the house and sometimes were paid for it. Unlike the children who received a regular amount of pocket money in return for housework, these children were only occasionally able to get a reward for work they did around the home. Money for housework was clearly mediated by the parents' capacity to pay for it:

> "I help mum around the house and she gives me a couple of pound now and then, so it's whatever she can afford you know." (Clarke, 15 years, lone-parent family)

Yet working in the home did not always mean that children received some money for it. Bella complained that she and her sister both did work around the house but still did not get any pocket money:

> "We do washing up every week and still she won't give us none." (Bella, 12 years, lone parent family)

Many of the children who did not receive pocket money were children who were doing some form of paid work outside of the home. Several of these children said that they used to receive pocket money in the past but were no longer receiving pocket money now they were working. However, many had not, making it difficult to separate whether children sought work through the necessity of not having pocket money, or gained work and then lost their pocket money entitlement. Previous research by Hutson and Cheung (1992) indicated that children aged 16-18 years were still given an allowance even where they were involved in Saturday or part-time work. So, for these low-income children, the initial lack of regular pocket money may well be one of the main factors driving their engagement in employment. For example, Nell used to have some pocket money before she was working but she found it very difficult to manage, and was now in regular work:

> "It was also for lunch and I buy my own things for school because I don't want to ask my parents, also I didn't really have very much money. I sometimes saved it up if I wanted something, but I would usually end up spending it all." (Nell, 17 years, two-parent family)

Children without access to regular income may well involve themselves in alternative strategies to gain access to money. In these instances children and young people may resort to stealing, shop lifting or other illegal activities. These were not reflected in these children's and young people's accounts. However, one of the fathers did report that his daughter had often stolen from the family when she was desperate for money. For some children, like Andy, pocket money was also intended to act as a supplement to school lunches. When he needed more money to go out he got round his shortage of money by saving and by creative use of his free school meals:

> "I used to get £1 a day, I think Monday to Friday, to go with my dinner and I used to, pretty much 'cos I got free school dinners, I used to save. I used to either save the pound and eat the meal or save the pound and occasionally I used to go in with the free school meal to buy food then sell it back out on the playground if I was like planning on going anywhere." (Andy, 16 years, two-parent family)

Evidently, there are several possible reasons why some children were not receiving any pocket money. First, it was apparent that a change in a family's circumstances, through sickness and disability, or through family break-up, could result in a change in economic well-being, whereby some of those children who had received pocket money in the past find that they were no longer able to have it. Second, it is clear that many parents were just too hard up to find regular extra money for their children, and here children themselves show a subtle understanding that there was literally not enough to go round. Finally, there was a clear link between working children and the lack of pocket money.

Parental perceptions of pocket money

We have heard from the children that very few were able to be sure of getting pocket money regularly. Here those parents who were interviewed (17) were asked how they felt about pocket money for their children. Studies of parental attitudes and values regarding pocket money and allowances show that most parents are in favour of giving pocket money. Recent research by Furnham (2001) found that 91% of parents believed that children from six years old onwards should have a regular weekly pocket money allowance. However, few of the parents in this study were able to provide any, and, as Dana pointed out, for many parents pocket money was not high on the list of necessities in a constrained budget:

> "Well they don't always get it, it depends really, if I've got it then I try and give it to 'em but obviously you can't do it all can you, it's obviously more important to put food in their mouths than give them money to throw away on sweets isn't it really. You know it's not something I wouldn't like to do but you got to put the most important things first haven't you." (Dana, lone parent)

For large families, it was impossible to provide something regularly for each child. Ivan had not given his four children pocket money for some time and he explained that this had occasionally led to stealing in his family, particularly by his oldest daughter, who was struggling to keep up with her friends:

"We get a bit of a problem with stealing from time to time.... It's a bit difficult, um, because it's all very well climbing in but at the end of the day you have a situation where you know why it's happening, so you've got to try and deal with it on that basis. She's in competition with families where 20 quid pocket money was nothing and it's so unfair." (Ivan, two-parent family)

Overall, the impression given by parents was that, while they would like to give their children pocket money, it was not possible given their current budgetary constraints.

Work: as a source of income

Children in the UK are working in increasing numbers, and overall it was estimated that over 70% of school children have worked at some time during their school careers (McKechnie et al, 1996). Although we know that a high percentage of children and young people work, the situation of children on a low income is less clear. There is some indication that children of middle-class parents may be more likely than children from poorer families to work (Morrow, 1994; Hobbs and McKechnie, 1997), although when children in poorer families do work they may take on more jobs and work for longer hours (Middleton et al, 1997). However, Mizen et al (1999) argue that most of the evidence available was contradictory and uncertain. Given the ambiguity surrounding our understanding of children in poverty and work, this study provides a valuable opportunity to listen to the experiences of low-income children and young people themselves.

Of the 40 children in the sample, 13 were currently in work, and five had been in work, making 18 children in the sample that were either working or had had experience of working. The legal age for work is 13 years old, and there were 18 children in the sample who were aged 13 years and above. Of these children, 12 had experienced work, eight were currently in work, and four had been in work and were still looking for work; of the remainder, only two young people said they were not looking for work. The majority of those children not working were below the legal age for work and for most of these children work was something they had not really considered yet.

Children who were currently working

Children and young people were employed in a variety of jobs. Dividing the type of jobs they did into formal (employed by a business or company), and informal (work for neighbours), a few children had informal employment (babysitting, grass cutting and gardening), and the majority of the others worked for formal employers (paper rounds, cleaning, shop work and so on). As in previous studies, a strong gender bias was evident (Lavalette, 1994; Leonard, 1998), with girls working mainly in babysitting, restaurants and shop work, and boys in paper rounds. However, two boys were doing cleaning jobs at their schools, an area that could traditionally be considered a female gendered job. Young people worked a range of hours per week, from a few hours a week babysitting to about 15 hours a week on cleaning and paper rounds. In general, hours increased with age, and a few young people were doing two jobs a week and working quite long hours. Two boys were working in their schools cleaning for two hours every night and they each also had additional jobs (one a paper round every morning and the other a Saturday job).

Problems with working

Time spent at work was time away from social life, family life and school commitments, and there was clearly a tension between the need and desire to work on the one hand, and finding time and energy to do so on the other. Children already experience a 30-hour week at school, and although schoolwork is most commonly dismissed as not work, Qvortrup (1985) points out that it is compulsory, and where children may benefit from their time at school, society also benefits from their application to study. Increasing homework demands will also have an impact on children's lives, especially where they are working. Several children expressed worries about balancing schoolwork, homework and leisure time; for one girl it meant that she had given up work until she had done her exams. For Andy it meant a complex juggling act between work, school and friends, and he feared that he may be compromising his schoolwork at a critical time:

> "Because I work quite a few hours more than they advise and plus I know people who don't, if they want to go out they do their work while I'm working for money and then they want to go out when I've just finished working, which doesn't give me much time to do my work in." (Andy, 16 years, two-parent family)

One girl, Laura, had given up work because she was afraid that her schoolwork would suffer. She had found life at school very hard and felt that she was being singled out as someone who would not succeed at school. This left her with a dilemma at work because although it gave more immediate access to having her own money, her long-term intention was to ensure that she did not have to manage on a low income in the future, like her mother. Her responses revealed some of the tensions that are apparent between paid work and maintaining an adequate performance at school:

> "I did used to have a job but it was interfering with my school life so I quit that ... I want to show people that I can do well [at school]. Like some people think that I can't do that well but I want to prove to people that I can do well." (Laura, 15 years, lone-parent family)

Why do children and young people work?

Extended periods of poverty may create a very particular relationship between these children and work, and the interviews provided a valuable opportunity to explore the role of employment in their lives, and the meanings and values they derived from it.

Money for social life and possessions

Children highlighted several key aspects of work, particularly autonomy, independence and choice. Amy highlighted the importance of work for her as a social as well as an economic issue. She liked to have her own independence and freedom; in particular for her, work also gave her entry into a valuable social environment:

> "I like working because I like being independent and I know I've worked hard for that money and I can go out and spend it.... I like it because I can go into town and buy a top and I think 'I've worked really hard for that'. It's not like brilliant money, that's 'cos of my age, but it's like I've got friends at work as well and well I just like working." (Amy, 15 years, two-parent family)

However, low-income children, while clearly active agents, are also severely constrained by their economic circumstances and this will impact on their capacity to exercise their choices about working or not working. As Mizen et al (2001) argue, children's motivations for working, like everyone else's, "express a relationship between choice and constraint, freedom and necessity" (Mizen et al, 2001, p 53). This was particularly apparent in low-income children's rationalisations about work. Employment represented an opportunity for freedom and independence; it also represented a key strategy in children's capacity to fulfil the normative social and economic expectations of their peer groups. In that sense it simultaneously freed them, to some degree, from the economic constraints of their family environment, and rendered them economic agents in their own right.

> "It really makes a big difference because I have an opportunity to buy things myself.... I can do things sometimes that I wouldn't have been able to do if I wasn't working because then I'd have to rely on my parents and I don't like to do that, I don't like to do that at all." (Nell, 17 years, two-parent family)

> "It helps me with money and school, and if I wanted to buy anything at the shops and that, or if we went to W... I could save it up for that. Yeah, it's made it a bit easier 'cos usually when I didn't have that I usually found it hard to get some money. Actually I felt more stuck at home than I do now." (Stewart, 16 years, lone-parent family)

However, economic necessity has meant that some children in the sample were 'choosing' to work at an early age. Kevin was below the legal age for work but he had found that work could make a considerable difference to his life, and he was determined to continue and get more work if possible. He explained why he was working, and what he planned to do:

> "[Before] I didn't have much money and I couldn't buy anything that I wanted ... [now] I get nine pounds a week and I can buy what I want with that basically and if I want anything for my bike I've got to save up for it.... I might be working in a restaurant this summer if I can, 'cos they took me and my friends' details down and we might be getting a job there soon." (Kevin, 12 years, lone-parent family)

Above all, the overriding impression given by children for working was the opportunity to gain access to their own financial resources and to experience the independence and autonomy that brought. Having their own money also gave them choices both socially and materially that they would not otherwise have had. For some of them, like Cherry, having their own income for the first time was profoundly liberating:

> "When I got my first wage packet I went out and blew it all in the first week, that was the first time I'd had lots of money of my own that I could do what I wanted with. But I learned from my mistakes 'cos I was skint for three weeks. I learned how to stretch it out over a four-week period." (Cherry, 17 years, lone-parent family)

However, although children had access to their own resources through work, these were rarely sufficient to sustain them adequately in the increasingly demanding consumer culture of their peers.

Money to ease pressure on parents

It was also clear that the children were not disengaging from the family economy, and several children in lone-parent families talked about lending their mothers money when they needed it. Where children did not in general appear to be contributing directly to the household budget, the contribution in kind through buying clothes and paying for their own social needs and so on, meant a valuable input to overall household budgets, freeing up money for other essential needs. Andy had been working for several years and had been in control of his own resources for some time:

> "I don't particularly like asking for money off dad, I mean I started a paper round when I was 14 and I have been working ever since, and so I pretty much paid for everything that I done." (Andy, 16 years, two-parent family)

Research has shown that even a relatively small amount of income could make a significant difference to the budgets of low-income families (Kempson, 1996); therefore, the contributions made by these children and young people in cash and in kind may be of considerable importance to their family's economic survival.

Children and young people without work

There were 10 children above the legal age for work who were not in work; only two of these young people indicated that they did not want to work. The other eight were all keen to get work and expressed several reasons for wanting work, not least for the social aspects of work, the money, and to stave off boredom at home. For several of the children, boredom at home was a key aspect of their desire to get out and do some work:

> "I might be getting a job down in the butchers down L... but that's hopeful. I don't know, it gets a bit boring some days so you've got something to do and you get some money in as well." (Clarke, 15 years, lone-parent family)

For rural children, the issue of finding work was particularly problematic. Lisa was concerned that she had not got a job and she felt that she needed to be able to have her own money; however, as she explained, where she lives in a small village there are no such opportunities for work:

> "I just want to have my own money. I'd like to be able to have a bit of pocket money to go out and buy my own stuff and not have to ask for money all the time, and be able to say I've worked for that money, and spend it because I feel good about it.... The problem [is] if I wanted to work in Y... and get a Saturday job it's too far to travel each day and I can't expect dad ... and if I wanted to get a bus that was £1.30 there, just there, which was quite a lot." (Lisa, 15 years, two-parent family)

Lisa's account highlights the tension between the desire to work and children's ability to access work, in terms of employment availability and access to transport; particularly for this group of rural children who were already disadvantaged by a lack of private transport. Sian highlighted the difficulties attendant on trying to get work in rural areas; she did not get pocket money and her mum had told her that if she wanted to have her own things she must go out to work and get her own money. However, there were few opportunities open to her and the cost of travelling outside her village was prohibitive. She had already tried to do some casual work tomato picking but left because she hated it:

> "I quit because it was horrible.... It was all older people about 30 or 40 and they were really ignorant, no one spoke to you and it was like huh! Great! ...

We've only got one shop and they've got all the people they need out there and I'm too young to be a bar steward up the club so that wouldn't work, so...." (Sian, 16 years, two-parent family)

Problems with working

Many of the opportunities children had for employment had come from small service sector employers. In small catering firms, children provide a cheap source of flexible labour, often working long hours and having low expectations of work (Mizen et al, 2001). Brad had taken on work in a chip shop but found that the hours were too long and irregular. He was often expected to work late at night and this was affecting his one social passion, which was to go out bike racing with his friends on Sundays. His account highlights many of the difficulties that children and young people face in an employment environment in which they have little power or protection against long or late hours and low rates of pay. He had asked to change his hours but had been told that if he wanted to keep his job he had to do longer hours and at a reduced rate. Here he explained why he decided to leave:

> "It never used to be £1.50 an hour, it used to be £2.50, £3, but after Christmas they just said right you're going to be working for £1.50 the hour and you're working these times. And I was going to ask them not to be having to work on a Saturday night because I used to have to work on a Saturday night from 10 till 1 in the morning, and when I used to race on Sunday I used to be like hanging, I couldn't race properly. And they wanted me to work on a Friday night from 10 till 1 and on a Saturday night from 10 till 1 and Sunday night from 10 till 1 and I don't want to do it so I just said no." (Brad, 15 years, two-parent family)

The value of work

For those children and young people who were working or seeking work, it was clearly highly prized. Although their experiences of work might be tiring, boring or demanding, overall the capacity to access money and the independence and autonomy that came with the money were invaluable. However, taken as a whole, it was apparent that for these children from low-income families there was no overall secure and reliable source of income. Rather, children were accessing money in a variety of ways. As Table 3.2 shows, only 11 children were able to rely on pocket money, which, as we have seen, may be from diverse sources and conditional. Thirteen children were working, and of these, only one child still received pocket money when he was working. It was apparent that these children had either entered work because they did not receive pocket money, or had experienced the withdrawal of their pocket money

Table 3.2: Children's access to financial resources via pocket money and work

	All	Gender		Family type	
		Girls	Boys	Lone-parent	Two-parent
Pocket money only	11	6	5	5	6
Work only	12	5	7	7	5
Both work and pocket money	1	0	1	1	0
Neither work *nor* pocket money	16	8	8	7	9
Base (100%)	40	19	21	20	20

Source: Ridge (2000)

once they started work. Nevertheless, they at least had access to some financial resources, whereas 16 children had no regular access to autonomous financial resources at all. These children appear to be particularly disadvantaged, having neither the security of regular pocket money payment, nor the capacity at present to earn money through their own work.

Parental views about children working

In families where children and young people had got work it was clearly appreciated by parents, although some expressed concern at the time then taken away from schoolwork. Several parents mentioned the value of their children providing for their own needs. Christine was a lone parent with four daughters; her oldest daughter was working and Christine was pleased that she was now able to buy her own toiletries and stationery for school. This also included buying her own sanitary wear which, with so many girls in the house, was a major expense every month. For Carol and Noleen, who are lone parents with three or four children to support, there were considerable benefits from their older children getting work and contributing towards the household expenses. As Noleen explained, she was unable to provide any of her children with pocket money, so while her daughter was now able to provide for some of her own needs, she was also able to help tide the whole family over through 'rough patches':

> "They don't have any [pocket money], they just don't have it, I try to give 'em what I can when I can. C... baby-sits so she does get her own money, she does it most weeks and she's very good, if I'm short she'll give it to me, she gets it back you know." (Noleen, lone parent)

Transport: as a key to social involvement

Most adults with adequate incomes expect mobility as a matter of course, and enjoy considerable freedom and access both within and beyond their immediate surroundings. Children, in contrast, tend to experience limited personal mobility and are heavily reliant on adults to supply their needs. Children in low-income families suffer the double disadvantage of being reliant on adults who are themselves often unable to meet their own or their family's transport needs.

In the previous two sections we have looked at children's restricted access to economic resources; we now focus on material resources, and look at the importance of transport for children. Of the 40 children in the sample, just over half lived in families who had their own vehicle. Table 3.3 shows that children living in two-parent families were more likely to live in a family where there was a car than were children in lone-parent families. The higher number of lone-parent families without a car may well reflect the gendered nature of lone parenthood and the likelihood that women are less likely to be able to drive, and may not have been left a vehicle in the division of property that follows relationship break-up. The difference between family types was particularly marked in rural areas. All rural two-parent families had access to a car, but only 3 out of 10 children living in rural lone-parent families did. This was a considerable disadvantage for rural children in lone-parent families as sustaining social relationships in rural areas was particularly dependent on personal mobility. Overall, rural children were more likely to live in a family with a car than urban children, half of whom had access to a car and half of whom did not. Even so, rural children in lone-parent families were the least likely of all children in the sample to have access to a car.

The costs of using private transport

Although some children lived in families where there was a car, the issue of whether or not they were able to take advantage of that fact was problematic due to petrol costs and dependence on adults for lifts. The scarcity of affordable public transport, particularly in rural areas, can mean that children are heavily dependent on their parents for their transportation needs, and transport can easily become an area of conflict, particularly when resources are scarce (Davis and Ridge, 1997). Negotiations between parents and children can be fraught, and it was apparent that several children and young people in the sample were restricting their own transport needs wherever possible to avoid pressurising their parents for lifts or for transport money. Nell explained that even though her parents have transport she was reluctant to ask them for lifts:

> "I don't like asking my parents to give me lifts to places because they are poor and they can't afford the petrol, and so I don't really like asking and if I do then I will generally pay for the petrol." (Nell, 17 years, two-parent family)

Table 3.3: Children's access to private transport, by family type and location

	Car	No car	Total
All	23	17	40
Lone-parent	9	11	20
Two-parent	14	6	20
Rural	13	7	20
Urban	10	10	20
Rural lone-parent	3	7	10
Rural two-parent	10	0	10
Urban lone-parent	6	4	10
Urban two-parent	4	6	10

Source: Ridge (2000)

Harry and Sian both live in rural areas, and found that getting to see their friends was difficult even though they had access to a car:

> "My mum doesn't drive, my dad's normally home 'cos he's not working ... if not then I'm stuck in T... really I'm stuck here." (Sian, 16 years, two-parent family)

> "Well it's horrible, everyone I know was from C.... Like you know. So I don't get out much. I've always like got to walk over to C... to get there or something, or I ask my mum to take me over in the car, she says no you can walk over or you can wait until later. If I wait till later then it's too dark." (Harry, 14 years, lone-parent family)

Children without access to a car

Many children and young people did not have any access to a private vehicle, the majority of them lived in lone-parent families and several remarked that their mothers could not drive. Most of these children used public transport where it was available and some were able to tap into help from their wider families, especially grandparents and their mother's boyfriends:

> " 'Cos my mum don't drive we usually go on the bus if we want to go into town or somewhere. Or sometimes if we don't want to go very far we walk." (Peter, 12 years, lone-parent family)

> "No, we ain't got no transport, we usually rely on my granddad 'cos mum don't drive and dad don't live here." (Clarke, 15 years, lone-parent family)

"Well my mum's boyfriend he lives at his house, but when he comes up if we want to go out places he takes us." (Sue, 11 years, lone-parent family)

Children and young people also showed a keen awareness of how costly public transport was, particularly when they were living as part of a large family. Charlene has three brothers and sisters, and she explained how any visits she makes with her family are very costly:

"Say if we all wanted to go out somewhere we have to pay quite a lot 'cos it's dear. 'Cos if we have to go to my nan's we have to pay about £10 or somethin' on the bus just to go over there." (Charlene, 12 years, lone-parent family)

The high cost of public transport was an important consideration to people on a low income and can easily result in an inability to make use of what public transport there is. For many of the children, the cost of travelling was having an effect on their ability to socialise with their friends, and, critically, it was constraining their capacity to join in and regularly attend clubs and other social activities. Nicole and Colleen were very aware that their friends were able to meet up and go out together on a more regular basis than they were able to join in with:

"My friends don't really live on this estate, only one, the others all live over F... and it's like quite far away and the bus fares are expensive and it's quite a walk." (Nicole, 13 years, lone-parent family)

"We usually do things together really, but most of my friends have got more transport than I have, more cars and things like that, so they can usually go different places." (Colleen, 13 years, lone-parent family)

Carrie rarely got to see her friends out of school because she was unable to pay the bus fare to see them:

"They live so far away and I can't get to them and they can't get to me 'cos it's like so much money on the bus to get to their homes, it's like really expensive." (Carrie, 15 years, lone-parent family)

Feeling excluded from after-school clubs because of transport difficulties was a particular issue for rural children who are bussed considerable distances to their schools, and find that without school transport to return home they are unable to stay on for after-school activities with their peers (Davis and Ridge, 1997). Peter had wanted to stay on at school and go to after-school clubs with his friends for some time but he was always constrained by whether or not another child from his village was going to stay on as well:

"Usually I get a lift home with somebody from school, so if they are not doing it [the club] then I'm a bit stuck getting home." (Peter, 12 years, lone-parent family)

Young people can find that access to buses and trains becomes even more difficult when they are older, particularly with regard to the differences between an adult and child's fare. For some, travelling on public transport becomes an area of tension and dispute:

"I can never go on for a child any more, they won't let me go on for a child. I always got to argue with them to let me on for a child and most of the time I just end up getting kicked off the bus for being older." (Brad, 15 years, two-parent family)

In rural areas, access to public transport was highly problematic. Buses can be scarce, irregular, and particularly expensive. Peter lives in a rural area with his mother, and he talked about how much he would like to go into town more, but that there were few buses and also that the cost was prohibitive:

"There's not much buses, 'cos we can't get in on Sundays and the bus fare was a bit high. So it's a bit of a waste of money [to] keep getting the bus in and the bus out." (Peter, 12 years, lone-parent family)

The high cost of travelling on buses and trains was compounded by constraints on money within families that affect pocket money and the possibility of any additional money for travel.

Parents' perceptions of transport

For the parents who were interviewed, ensuring that they had adequate transport for their overall needs was an ongoing concern. Among those families where there was a parent or a child with a disability, the need for transport was particularly acute, especially if, like Melanie, they were living in a rural area. For these families, private transport was a necessity, not a luxury. Melanie explained that a regular bus route did not serve the rural estate that she lives on, and they have had to make other sacrifices to ensure that they are able to run a car:

"Just doing things like going to the dentist, my husband has got a disability so I have to take him to the doctors quite regularly, you know, without a car we couldn't manage." (Melanie, two-parent family)

Lone-parent families were the least likely to have transport, and for rural lone parents this was particularly problematic. Many of them, like Diane and Nicola, had not retained access to the family car when they had separated from their partners. Nicola explained how she had lost access to the car, and was having difficulties keeping her children in touch with their Nan, who was in a nursing home:

> "I think that's what I miss most about my husband was the car.... It's very expensive, 'cos my mum's in a nursing home and I go and see her twice a week and it costs me six pounds, so that's six pounds out of my money straight away. You know and she does try and give it back to me as much and often as she can, but she hasn't got a lot of money so she, you know, she tries to give me the odd pound here and there. If I take one of the children that's five pounds straight away so they don't get to see their nan very much." (Nicola, lone parent)

Trudy and Diane also talked about how they were unable to take their children out for any trips because of the cost of using public transport, and then the inevitable extra costs of the day out itself. For Diane, lack of transport meant a heavy reliance on her boyfriend for help; without him, the costs of the buses were too prohibitive for trips out:

> "I just can't afford the price of bus fares to be honest ... by the time you paid your bus fare you got nothing to spend when you get there." (Diane, lone parent)

Trudy was angry because she felt that even though she was living in a rural area and relatively close to the sea, she was still unable to take advantage of the possibility of a free day out because of the high cost of travelling to get there. She was unhappy about never feeling able to take her children out for the day:

> "Not being able to take them anywhere, you know 'cos if you just say 'Oh we'll go down to W...', you've got to make sure you've got petrol to get there, and then they always want something when you're there, whether it's a burger or ... and it adds up so we just don't." (Trudy, two-parent family)

When adults talked about transport they did so in the context of their overall family needs rather than in relation to the needs of their children in particular. Everyday issues of access to affordable resources and services are constant and demanding preoccupations for parents managing on a low income. As such, there may be little time or energy to engage with the extra social needs of their children, particularly in the light of their inability, in many cases, to manage and to afford their family's most basic transport needs. This was also true of pocket money, where a parent's prime consideration lies in managing a restricted family budget to sustain overall family needs, rather than in responding to children's needs for autonomous economic resources.

Summary

Children's interaction with the economic world is increasing, and early experience of managing pocket money is considered an important element in economic socialisation. We live in an increasingly complex economy and children are significant consumers from an early age. Annual monitoring of pocket money receipts by Wall's shows that Britain's children (aged 5-16 inclusive) have a total weekly spending power of approximately £60 million (Wall's, 2001), and almost all children from the age of nine upwards have their own money to spend (ChildWise, 2001). However, listening to children in this study reveals that for them pocket money was not an expectation, but rather a scarce and vital resource, one which, when available, enabled them to share in the everyday culture of their friends, and also gave them the opportunity to have some control over money in the face of a particularly constrained economic environment. Overall, of the 40 children sampled, only nine children received regular unconditional pocket money.

Children who were not receiving any pocket money highlighted how lack of personal and autonomously controlled income was a severe disadvantage in their social lives. For these children and young people, paid work appeared to be a necessary objective, and it was apparent that where pocket money was not forthcoming, work was playing a major role in sustaining children's financial needs. However, of particular concern must be those children who were without pocket money or work. They appear to be particularly disadvantaged, having neither the small measure of freedom and social viability that comes with pocket money, nor the capacity to access their own autonomous resources from work.

When children and young people were working, this clearly played an essential role in providing a measure of autonomy and security. Money earned was used to participate with other children and young people, to share in social events and to save and purchase important signifiers of childhood social status, such as clothes or trainers. Income from work both sustains children and contributes to family budgets directly and in kind. Paradoxically, work was also shown to have a negative impact on children's lives, through low pay, loss of time for social interaction, and tensions between school and work, which had caused several children and young people to leave their employment. These issues pose hard policy questions about the role of work in the lives of children experiencing poverty over a long duration.

It was also clear that access to affordable transport was an especially vital issue for children from low-income families; without it they are particularly vulnerable to social, and in some instances, spatial, isolation. Nearly half of the sample lived in households without a car, and the majority of these were living in lone-parent households. The difference between lone- and two-parent households was particularly marked in rural areas, where access to a car was generally considered an essential need rather than a luxury item. Rural areas tended to be characterised by a paucity of public transport provision, which was likely to be expensive and poorly targeted at the needs of children and young people.

While the parents who were interviewed showed a keen awareness of the costs of transport and its impact on them as a family, they appeared to be less aware of the impact of costly or scarce transport on children themselves and their capacity to see friends. This was understandable in the context of families' greater priorities to ensure that they are able to get food, access services and ensure that their children go to school. It was also in line with a general adult perspective that rarely considers transport as a pressing issue for children. However, it was clear from children's accounts that transport was an important concern and one which had a particular impact on their capacity for sustaining an acceptable level of social involvement.

The realities for children in this study are clear; their parents simply do not have sufficient income to provide the things that children themselves identify as essential for secure social interaction with their peers. In the next chapter, we will explore in more detail the social demands of childhood, and how children view their social relationships at home and at school.

Notes

[1] See Shropshire and Middleton (1999) for research into children's receipt of pocket money using a child's questionnaire.

[2] Social class D was defined as working class – semi and unskilled manual workers; and social class E was defined as those at the lowest subsistence level (state pensioners and so on), with no other earnings (Lewis, 2001).

FOUR

'Fitting in' and 'joining in': social relations and social integration

Chapter Three revealed the tangible impact of economic and material poverty on the lives of children from low-income families. However, to understand the multidimensional impact of poverty on children's lives, an analysis of poverty that embraces the social relational aspects of children's lives is also needed. The notion of social exclusion has the potential to broaden our understanding of poverty from a narrow issue of inadequate material resources to a more comprehensive and dynamic analysis (Berghman, 1995). The relational impact of poverty, outlined by Room (1995), as inadequate social participation, lack of social integration and lack of power has a particular resonance in children's lives. Childhood is a social experience in itself, with its own norms and customs, where the costs of inclusion may be great, likewise the cost of exclusion. Friendships and social interactions with peers are key locations where children develop their social identity and enhance their social capital. This chapter provides an opportunity to understand the social lives and experiences of children in poverty, through the medium of their own voices. It reveals the children's interpretations and constructions of their social relationships and it explores the children's perceptions of their ability to participate in the social world of their peers.

The chapter focuses on three key areas:

- The capacity of children to *fit in* with their peers. This is examined through an exploration of social relationships bounded by friendship and bullying.
- The importance of *clothes* as a key signifier of peer inclusion, this was a particular area of concern identified by children during the interviews.
- Children's opportunities to *join in* shared social activities with their peers. This focuses in particular on children's social experiences at school and on the children's perceptions of their capacity to join in with shared social activities.

'Fitting in': friendships

The importance of friendships and the value of developing and sustaining satisfactory social relationships have only recently been acknowledged as significant factors in the development of social capital and in the maintenance of secure social identities. With modern society increasingly characterised by risk and uncertainty (Beck, 1992), the value of friendships as a source of support in the face of breakdown of other traditional forms of support has only recently been explored (Pahl and Spencer, 1997; Pahl, 1998; Silva and Smart, 1999). In a complex and demanding social environment, friendships and informal relationships can act as a 'social glue', binding us into the social structure (Jerrome, 1984). Friendships, and by extension social networks, are also increasingly recognised as powerful social assets, playing an important role in the development and maintenance of social capital (Pahl and Spencer, 1997; Pahl, 2000). 6 (1997) has argued that 'network poverty', a lack of secure social networks, can play a critical role in people's vulnerability to poverty and social exclusion.

Friendship for children has generally been seen as an essential part of cultural reproduction, and the development of secure social identities (Rubin, 1980; James et al, 1998). The importance of friendship for children lies not just in the growth and development of social skills and social identity, but also in learning to accept and understand others. Children need to learn not just how to make friends, but also crucially how to be a friend (Furnham, 1989). However, friendship for children, as for adults, also creates an entry point into wider social relationships; it plays a role as a social asset — a source of social capital — both in childhood and in the future. Conversely, difficulties in maintaining social relationships can leave children vulnerable to social exclusion (see Ridge and Millar, 2000).

An exploration of the meaning and value of friendships among children from low-income families may provide an important insight into the role of friendships in children's well-being and social integration. Previous research has shown that friendships can have diverse meanings for children (James, 1993; Brannen et al, 2000), and this was reflected in the variety of different reasons that children in this study gave about why they felt friendship was important. As well as the more obvious reasons for children valuing friends for play and sociability, they also identified considerably more complex reasons.

The value of friends

As with previous research, the friendships in this study were strongly gendered (Archer, 1992; Hartup, 1992; James, 1993; Jamieson, 2001). Girls were generally more articulate about their friendships, and were much more likely to see friends as confidants and as supportive and valued alternatives to family. Boys were more likely to see friendship as an opportunity for having fun and a good time, but they also valued the protective effect of friendship in the face of bullying. These are in line with Hartup's findings (1992), that girls' relationships tend to be more 'intensive' and boys' more 'extensive'.

For many children, having the companionship of friends ensured fun and happiness. This was a view of friendship that was more likely to be articulated by the boys, although the girls also appreciated good times with friends. Friends staved off boredom and without friends, they felt they would not be happy:

"Like if you ain't got no one to speak to or anything then it will be like sort of borin' and all that. If you've got a problem and you ain't got anybody to speak to, if you've got a friend then you 'ave and they can sort things as well." (Cally, 14 years, two-parent family)

"I go round my friends' houses quite a lot and there would be no one to talk to and I would get really bored if I had no friends." (Kevin, 12 years, lone-parent family)

Although friends were undeniably valued for fun and enjoyment, many children and young people identified the importance of friendship as a source of social and emotional sustenance. This was an aspect of friendship that was articulated most often by girls. For many children and young people, the family is not necessarily the ideal site for sharing problems; alternative sites of support are sought and often found in friendships:

"They are as important as your family especially when you are this age, because your family can help you to a certain extent but for the things you don't want to tell your family, friends are so important to have." (Amy, 15 years, two-parent family)

"It's someone to talk to and rely on, and go out with.... Some things that happen[s] you can't just go along and tell your mum, can you, or your dad, and say like this happened." (Colleen, 13 years, lone-parent family)

Friends were supportive and discrete confidants, and reciprocity played an important part in maintaining and nurturing friendships:

"Just to talk to and to tell 'em things and you know they are going to keep it a secret, not tell anyone else." (Charlene, 12 years, two-parent family)

"Like I'm there for them and they're there for me, and we're all really close and get on really well, and I just think its really important." (Carrie, 15 years, lone-parent family)

For many of the children, friendship also performed a valuable social function, averting the dangers of loneliness and social isolation. Clarke summed up the general feeling:

"If you haven't got friends you haven't got a lot really have you, you know." (Clarke, 15 years, lone-parent family)

Protection from bullying

Lacking friendships is one of the key risk factors for being a victim of bullying (Boulton et al, 1999; Pellegrini et al, 1999), and children showed a keen awareness that to be friendless was to be vulnerable and exposed:

> "If you're lonely you can get teased and they say that you are a lemon or a loner." (Sal, 12 years, lone-parent family)

> "If you don't have any [friends] you won't be able to go out and play without being bullied." (Jim, 10 years, two-parent family)

The protective factor of friendships was also apparent from some of the children's accounts; their friends had helped them at school to avert the attention of bullies or to mediate between them and their teachers:

> "When someone is just like beating you up, you've got like someone next to you to stand up for you as well." (Nigel, 10 years, two-parent family)

> "If you are getting bullied you can't tell the teacher, they just, they will go and tell for you.... I got bullied once and I couldn't go and tell the teacher and then like Jamie went to go and tell." (Adam, 10 years, two-parent family)

Friendships bring wider social networks

Friendships also open the door to other relationships with friends' parents and siblings, a whole social milieu. For some children this was particularly valuable where their own home life was stressed, or where they were socially restricted. Lisa spent every weekend away from home that she could, staying with her friends and their families:

> "It gives me a break from here as well, 'cos we're not like the perfect family who get on all the time and stuff. Because it's been hard with [step-mother's] children and her, and her way of living and us mixing in.... There are like the arguments and the rows, especially at my age and being a teenager and stuff. So it's nice to be able to get out ... 'cos it's like a different living." (Lisa, 15 years, two-parent family)

It was evident from the children's accounts that they valued friendship highly, and that it performed several important social functions for them; many of the functions belie the everyday simplistic impressions of children's friendships as mere extensions of playground society. However, although their perceptions of friendship involved feeling happy, secure and supported, their social realities were very different. Many of the children were experiencing bullying and problems making and sustaining their friendships.

Bullying

Previous research has shown that around one quarter of children have been bullied in school (Whitney and Smith, 1993). Bullying can affect children's self-esteem and social values; it may also affect learning (Smith and Sharp, 1994) and lead to truancy (Carlen et al, 1992). Nearly half of the children talked about being bullied, either currently or in the past. This had had a marked effect on how they felt about their school and, in some cases, about themselves. There was no substantial difference between gender or by family type. However, there were signs of difference between rural and urban locations. Rural children seemed more likely to report having been bullied – 14 rural compared to five urban children. This may well reflect different school practices, or the possibility that children from families on a low income stand out more in a rural environment than urban children from low-income families. Most of the bullying revolved around school where children came into regular contact with their peers. Nell suffered years of bullying at her school and highlighted the importance of developing secure friendships for protection and improved self-esteem:

> "I used to get bullied constantly because of my attitude to things.... If you're not entirely confident about your appearance then people are bound to pick on you. It was one of my friends who stopped me from being bullied because she was trying to build my confidence up for ages." (Nell, 17 years, two-parent family)

Some of the children in the study had been bullied for several years, and had developed strategies to protect themselves:

> "If you haven't got a friend in school you feel more lonely, and you feel like sometimes school work can be much harder.... I was bullied for a couple of years but I got used to it and ignored 'em and got on with my work." (Stewart, 16 years, lone-parent family)

Children who were being bullied had little faith in the school system or in its ability to stop their unhappiness. One 10-year-old had reported his bullying at school but nothing had been done about it. Another felt that there was nobody he could tell. Bella was particularly unhappy and wanted to change her school:

> "I want to change to a new school, because I don't like it up there no more. I got bullied and well, the police officer used to come and see me, and a girl found out and she's told everyone at the school, now I just want to move school." (Bella, 12 years, lone-parent family)

Her experiences at school had also undermined her confidence in her school friendships, which had left her feeling very isolated; she now felt she had no one to talk to if she had problems:

> "No I can't tell 'em 'cos they go and tell their friends or something." (Bella, 12 years, lone-parent family)

Transitions from one school to another can also be daunting for children who have been bullied. Milly had been bullied and did not like school because people were "horrible" to her; she was worried about what was going to happen to her when she went to secondary school:

> "Because you hear stuff like they flush your head down toilets and stuff, so I don't want to go." (Milly, 10 years, lone-parent family)

Difficulties making and sustaining friendships

As well as the experiences and fears of bullying, nearly half of the sample were experiencing difficulties either making or sustaining their friendships. There was an underlying assumption that all children have friends in their immediate neighbourhood; however, this was not reflected in children's accounts and 14 children said they did not have friends living nearby. They, along with four others (making nearly half of the sample), had difficulties in seeing school friends, and sustaining the friendships they had made at school. School friends lived too far away to meet after school, and the children in the sample found weekends and holidays quite isolating. Difficulties in accessing transport and the cost of transport were also major factors mentioned by children. In common with many of the children and young people in the study, Carrie rarely got to see her friends out of school because of problems with transport. She wished that she could move nearer to her school friends as she had no friends near to where she lived. Here she explained why she was never able to see her friends out of school:

> "Because they live so far away and I can't get to them and they can't get to me. 'Cos it's like so much money on the bus to get to their homes, it's really expensive." (Carrie, 15 years, lone-parent family)

Some children felt very isolated and did not feel that they had friends at home or at school. For them friendship was a shifting and insecure thing. Shamus had experienced the loss of friends and the social insecurity this can bring:

> "Once you lose one friend then you lose the rest of them." (Shamus, 12 years, lone-parent family)

Most of the children had friends but were experiencing great difficulty in maintaining their friendships in the way they thought fit. However, a few of the children appeared particularly socially isolated. Kim had very few friends, and was quite isolated in her home environment. Her family lived in a rural area and there had been some difficulty fitting into the neighbourhood. In general, she did not associate with the children in her area and spent little time outside of the house:

> "We sometimes play at the park, but without other kids.... I normally play on my own or with my brothers. I hardly ever play with them." (Kim, 11 years, lone-parent family)

For rural children, village life can also be isolating and children can find that they have few children of their own age living in their village. Children and young people are often bused long distances to their rural schools and, without adequate after-school transport, children from low-income families in particular are effectively trapped and contained within their villages (Davis and Ridge, 1998). Sian had few friends of her own age in the village and saw very little of her friends from school; she wished she could see them more:

> "I've got one [friend] that lives down the road, but she's two years younger than me, I've got no one really my age in the village." (Sian, 16 years, two-parent family)

One way in which children can see friends who live further away and develop their friendships was to have them to stay the night, quite a common practice in childhood. However, this was not possible for all the children and many of the children said that they were not able or allowed to have friends to stay. In some cases it was a question of space; they were living in crowded conditions and sharing bedrooms, where a visitor would be considered too much extra. For some of the children in the two-parent families, the special needs of the parent or child with a disability meant that having friends to stay was problematic. One of the parents explained how her children were increasingly restricted in their capacity to have friends over even to play:

> "I'd like to move to a bigger house, I know we've got a roof over our heads and we're very lucky in that respect ... but their father has got a progressive disease in his nervous system and he finds it difficult having them around sometimes, and we haven't really got anywhere they can sort of get away.... They're having to be quiet a lot of the time and not have their friends round so much as other kids do." (Jackie, two-parent family)

Without space and/or transport, the issue of reciprocity was raised. Parents may be reluctant to let children stay away from home with friends when they are unable to return the gesture. Having children to stay was also costly, and there are not always extra resources to go around. Kevin felt that having less money had made a difference to his friends when they came to stay:

> "They've got nicer houses than this one and they like found it cold when they stay in my house because I haven't got central heating." (Kevin, 12 years, lone-parent family)

Stability was important in maintaining friendships and moving can be very disruptive to children's social relationships. Bella had moved five times in her life, and found it very difficult to sustain supportive and lasting friendships. She also suffered from a painful period of bullying at school. She said she would not want to move again because she needed to make friendships that would last, and this was more likely if she could stay in one place:

> "I've moved so many times that I like to keep set on one place where I can make new friends, I like to stay here." (Bella, 12 years, lone-parent family)

The significance of friendship for children lies not just in the growth and development of social skills, but also in learning to accept and understand others and to foster social belonging and integration. It is a precious social asset, and one that many of these children and young people, through the effects of poverty and inadequate space and resources, are evidently finding it hard to sustain. The harsh realities of problematic peer relationships are bullying and exclusion. Ambert (1995) argues that bullying can happen simply because children "do not belong to the proper race, religion, social class, or, even do not wear 'appropriate' clothing, do not belong to the 'in' groups and do not share in the values and pastimes of their peers" (1995, p 186). The next section explores one of these factors, the need to wear the 'appropriate' clothing for peer acceptance.

'Fitting in': the importance of clothes

Young people use fashion and clothes as a means of making and expressing their identities (Willis et al, 1990). As children get older the relationship between peer inclusion and individuality becomes more complex (Miles, 1996), but for younger children the need to fit in and to feel part of the prevailing peer culture was strong. Previous research has shown that children are under considerable pressure to wear 'acceptable' clothes from an early age (Middleton et al, 1994).

In this study, children themselves identified the importance of clothes, and highlighted their efforts to maintain the 'right' appearance to fit in with their peers. They talked about their relationship with clothes, how important they felt clothes were, and what the implications were for them if they could not sustain an 'appropriate' appearance according to their peers. Carrie sets the scene:

"If you don't wear the right stuff you're like different and that of the crowd, just different. It's right to have the right clothes." (Carrie, 15 years, lone-parent family)

The majority of the children and young people felt that clothes were an important issue for them and those that did not were mainly younger children. Clothes appeared to be marginally more important for girls than for boys, and there were also signs that children in urban areas would be more likely to feel that clothes were important than rural children and young people. This may indicate that urban life might be more socially demanding for children. Age was an important factor in children's perceptions of clothes and the age of 12 seems to be a critical age for self-awareness and self-esteem. Colleen explained how she has changed over time, and how clothes are now much more important than when she was younger:

"When I was about 10 I didn't really care, I just went out and wore whatever, it didn't really matter. But as you grow up you're more conscious about what you're wearing and everything, as you get older it's different." (Colleen, 13 years, lone-parent family)

There were only five children over the age of 12 who were apparently unconcerned about clothes, and their responses revealed that this was not necessarily a comfortable area for them. Stewart was aware of the importance of clothes for self-image and acceptance but he was also realistic about what clothes he was able to afford:

"Some people, what you wear is more like what you are sort of thing. I try to keep myself looking kind of neat sort of thing, but 'cos I got no choice to wear certain clothes an' that.... I'm not really worried about what sort of names and things I wear, I just wear what I can get." (Stewart, 16 years, lone-parent family)

Why clothes are important

Children were very clear about why they felt that clothes were important, and several reasons were given for needing to have the 'right' clothes. Clothes were needed for children to be able to 'fit in' and be part of a social group. They were also identified as important for protection from bullying and exclusion. Children and young people also talked about the role of clothes in developing their self-esteem and building their confidence. These were not discrete reasons but interlocked and they reinforce each other. It was both reassuring and self-affirming for children to feel that they fitted into the social groups to which they aspired. Many children outlined the consequences of not having the right clothes, either for themselves, or for other children:

"If you don't wear trendy stuff … not so many people will be your friend 'cos of what you wear." (Charlene, 12 years, two-parent family)

"You've got to keep going with the trend otherwise you kind of get picked on kind of thing." (Peter, 12 years, lone-parent family)

"If they, like, have clothes that they had for quite a while and they've grown out of it, and be, like, sort of too short for them and all, then people call them tramps and smelly and all that." (Cally, 14 years, two-parent family)

As we have seen, the fear of being bullied was very real, and the flipside of being part of the group was being apart. Designer labels were particularly singled out as signifiers of fashion and inclusion, and this was clearly a difficult area to negotiate. Nicole and Amy outlined the perils of not having the right labels on your clothes:

"They might have trainers but it would be like, um, like Gola or something like, like really sad make, that people think are sad anyway. And they like get the mickey taken out of them." (Nicole, 13 years, lone-parent family)

"Some kids can be really cruel even about what you're wearing. It's sort of like they can be friends with someone and then disown them because they haven't got say Adidas track suit bottoms on." (Amy, 15 years, two-parent family)

Being fashionable was clearly considered important by some children; however, underlying the desire to be fashionable were also worries that their friends would have better clothes than them and the fear of being singled out and different:

"If you are like wearing fashion clothes people don't stare at you. If you are wearing like scruffy clothes people just go 'Look, look at him, scrub!', or something like that." (Kevin, 12 years, lone-parent family)

"You don't really want like not very nice things, you don't want like holey things. You want like nice clean things and new things. So you don't really want old things." (Nigel, 10 years, two-parent family)

Overall, children and young people did not mention the desire to have all designer label clothing, and this was in some part likely to be a realistic reflection of their inability to get them. Their concern was directed at ensuring that they did not make social gaffes and were not singled out in any way. On the whole, clothes seemed to be an area where these children struggled particularly hard to attain the things they felt that they needed. One child said he would not go out if he did not have the right clothes because he would be too embarrassed; another that he always made sure he had the right clothes.

The cost of clothes

Many of the children and young people who were not able to get the clothes they felt they needed were keenly aware that their parents could not afford them:

> "I would ask my parents to buy me things and then I realised that my parents couldn't afford things. 'Cos I'd sit down and listen to their conversations and then I stopped asking for things and saved up for them. And that's been ever since I was about D's age, since I was about eight, because I was a quick learner." (Nell, 17 years, two-parent family)

> "It's like all the fashion and like sports stuff and that. And it's really expensive and mum won't be able to afford it so I wouldn't be able to have it." (Nicole, 13 years, lone-parent family)

Clearly the cost of buying new clothes was prohibitive and children and young people were keenly aware of the cost; many had devised a variety of strategies to get the clothes. Some children would save up and buy their own clothes through catalogues, and for the young people who were working, this had made a considerable difference in their ability to get such clothes:

> "I'd rather buy for myself 'cos I like to be the same as my friends and my mum can't afford it. So I just save up for myself, so my mum don't have to pay." (Laura, 15 years, lone-parent family)

However, as we saw in the previous chapter, many children were not working and they were also not able to access regular pocket money to be able to save. For these children the disadvantages of having the wrong clothes appeared to be particularly acute:

> "I just want to fit in the group, 'cos it's like I get ..., people take the mick out of me because I can't afford things. Like my trainers are messy and they don't suit me and I need new trainers and new clothes ... I can't get decent clothes like everyone else does." (Bella, 12 years, lone-parent family)

> "If you haven't got the right clothes and all your friends have got all the nice clothes you feel left out like, 'cos like you think to yourself, 'Oh they've got all the good clothes and they've got all the money to buy them' and that and you feel left out.... I sometimes like get really worried if like I've got all these old fashioned clothes and I don't like them and everyone else has fashionable ones." (Sue, 11 years, lone-parent family)

Gaining confidence from looking good

Where children and young people had managed to dress in a way that pleased them and conformed to the prevailing fashion demands, they singled out the feelings of self-confidence and self-esteem that followed; looking good was an important part of feeling good:

> "It's all about my confidence really, if I feel good in what I'm wearing I can talk to people better and stuff." (Amy, 15 years, two-parent family)

> "I'm very fussy about clothes ... I don't know why but I can't go out and look horrible, 'cos I feel like people are watching me and that and I have to go out look presentable. I can't go out and look scruffy or anything like that. I won't go out if I look scruffy, I won't do it." (Colleen, 13 years, lone-parent family)

The importance of clothes, and in particular the capacity to wear the 'right' clothes, to maintain a degree of social acceptance within peer groups, has been plainly revealed. Children maintained that suitable standards of clothing were needed in order to 'fit in' and to feel part of their social groups. The disadvantages of not having the 'right' clothes were revealed through children's fears of isolation, bullying and exclusion. However, the cost of buying the 'right' clothes was prohibitive, and children showed a keen awareness of the tensions between needing to have the 'right' clothes and being able to afford them.

'Joining in': social experiences at school

Recent anti-poverty policy measures intended to address children's social and developmental needs have been directed mainly through school, and have focused almost entirely on improving literacy and numeracy standards (DSS, 1999b), and tackling truancy and school exclusions (SEU, 1998c). While these are critical and important issues in children's lives, the degree of social inclusion that children experience at school and at home is also vital. There is an underpinning assumption of parity of opportunity and experiences between children within school that is rarely challenged. There has been little interest or debate about the potential for education to be exclusionary and divisive between children and young people from low-income families and their more affluent peers.

Current education policy is increasingly driven by demands to improve academic standards. But school also plays a particularly significant role in children's lives as a site of social as well as pedagogical learning. There is increasing interest in school as an environment for developing 'soft skills'[1] for future employability. Children's learning intersects with their home and community environment, and this consequently leads to different experiences and outcomes (Pollard and Filer, 1996). Therefore, how children from low-income families experience school may well be mediated by the constraints of their home environment. Yet there is very little knowledge or understanding of how children in poverty might experience school, or the impact of low income on their school lives. This section explores with children their social experiences at school, and their capacity to engage with school life and participate in school social activities.

Feelings about school

Children and young people were asked whether or not they liked school, and the majority of children from the sample said that they did like school. However, over a quarter of the sample said that they did not like school or were ambivalent about it. Those that did not like school gave a variety of reasons, including because they were getting bullied, they did not like their teachers, or they found the work too demanding:

> "No I don't really like it that much because you get bullied and that." (Jim, 10 years, two-parent family)

> "I don't get on with many of the teachers 'cos my older two brothers went through that school and they set a bad reputation for me." (Brad, 15 years, two-parent family)

> "I used to like it, it's just too much to do now, getting ready for exams, it's boring." (Sian, 16 years, two-parent family)

Others were disappointed with school but endured it without liking it. Clarke's response was typical of these:

> "I just go and do what I've got to do but I don't like it." (Clarke, 15 years, lone-parent family)

However, when children talked about what they liked about school, by far the most popular response was that school was an opportunity to meet with friends. The greater parts of children's social interactions with other children are contextualised within the school environment, and children and young people who were unable to meet with their friends outside of school particularly valued the opportunity to associate with them in school:

> "That's mostly where I see them [friends] at school, or like I might see them in town, but apart from that I don't really see them." (Nicole, 13 years, lone-parent family)

For rural children, large catchment areas mean that children have few opportunities to meet up out of school, especially when they have no access to transport. Clarke did not like school but he did value it as a place where he could meet up with his peers, which was particularly difficult in the rural village where he currently lives:

> "I see most of my mates that I don't see round my village that are more of my age. But they don't live round here so I get to see them I suppose which is quite good." (Clarke, 15 years, lone-parent family)

School also allows children to make relationships with other adults, particularly teachers, and they played an important part in some children's accounts:

> "It's got loads of activities and the teachers are really kind." (Sal, 12 years, lone-parent family)

The majority of children in the sample had never been excluded from their schools, but three had been excluded from lessons or for the day from school, and one young child had been banned from going on school trips.

In their discussions about school and the quality of their school lives, the children and young people identified several areas of school life that were causing them concern. One of these was the issue of school uniforms and the difficulties children were having ensuring that they were able to conform with their school dress codes (see below).

School uniforms

The previous section has shown the importance attached to wearing the 'right' clothing, particularly for fitting into the social groups to which children and young people aspire. This awareness of clothing codes also extended to the school environment where children and young people spend a large part of their day in social interaction with their peers. The insistence of schools on a uniform has long been recognised as having a protective effect for children. However, although children acknowledged and confirmed the value of school uniform, they also revealed a sharp awareness of the subtler nuances of clothing codes that can override those protective effects. Several children pointed to things that could jeopardise that:

> "Well it's important to have a decent school uniform because like you see some people going there and they haven't got enough money to buy like the uniform so they are in like different things." (Sue, 11 years, lone-parent family)

> "[Uniform is] quite good yeah because they can't take the mick out of you if you've got like no named stuff. But you still 'ave to 'ave good trainers or good shoes." (Charlene, 12 years, two-parent family)

'Mufti day'

Children and young people also identified certain occasions when they were particularly vulnerable. One such occasion highlighted by many was 'mufti day' (a day free of school uniform), when they found it difficult to find the right clothes to wear, and in some cases were really anxious leading up to the day and on the day itself. The common experience was of not having enough of the 'right' clothes to wear:

> "Sometimes I don't know what to wear 'cos I ain't got much stuff." (Charlene, 12 years, two-parent family)

> "You spend about two weeks planning what you are wearing, discuss it with everyone just to make sure you are wearing the right things." (Carrie, 15 years, lone-parent family)

Amy found mufti day particularly worrying, and she explained why she was so against having them at school:

> "When I was younger I wore something in one time, and then a couple of months later we had another non-uniform day, I wore it again and I was worried about that but no one noticed. But I was very 'Oh my God, what if everyone notices I've worn it twice sort of thing.... I don't think [we] should have to pay for non-uniform days. In fact, I don't think we should have non-uniform days. Because I like the idea of a uniform 'cos everyone's the same and you ain't got to worry about what other people are wearing and it's so much better. I just don't think it's right." (Amy, 15 years, two-parent family)

As well as needing to ensure that they had the 'right' kind of uniform and shoes, there were other demands on children and their families to provide school bags, equipment and stationery:

> "People were always on top of each other like 'Oh you've got that bag, why haven't you got Umbro or Nike or something like that'. Which I did 'cos I would make sure dad would like get them for me. I wouldn't be out." (Lisa, 15 years, two-parent family)

> "Like we've got to work out all this money for school bags and stationery, and then you've got a uniform that when it gets too small for you as well you've got to keep paying every two years or something. It gets expensive." (Nicole, 13 years, lone-parent family)

School trips

A further area of disadvantage identified by children and young people from low-income families at school were their opportunities to go on school trips with their class mates. School trips are an important part of shared school life, providing an opportunity for social contact and different life experiences. With an increasingly demanding exam curricular, there are a growing number of opportunities to go on trips to enhance school work, including trips to theatres, museums, textile and fashion shows and so on. There are also opportunities for social events such as days out at amusement parks or camping weeks. Andy was clear that attendance on school trips was an important part of school life, and there were social repercussions for those who were unable to go:

> "I think it was quite important 'cos you miss out. It's a very social thing to do especially if a group has like a day of school and the people who are left behind in the school are the people who are looked down on." (Andy, 16 years, two-parent family)

The value of school trips

School trips are also an opportunity to have a break from everyday lessons and for the children to develop different shared social experiences with friends. For those children who had gone on school trips, the experience was clearly a valued one. Sian had been able to go on a trip with her school to Germany, and she thought everything about it was special:

> "Everything, I had time with my friends, I was in a different country, away from my mum and dad." (Sian, 16 years, two-parent family)

Amy was not able to go on trips very often but here she talks about one trip she had which she described as a really big treat; it was to the Clothes Show, and was particularly important for her because she was studying textiles in her GCSE exams:

> "I was so excited about going and I saved up some money to get some stuff, and mum and dad says like 'Right 'cos it's like you really want to go, we'll treat you'. And I was so happy about it. And I got there and I was like 'Oh this means so much'. 'Cos it was like a really big treat for me, and I come back and I couldn't stop talking about it for days." (Amy, 15 years, two-parent family)

Some schools were able to provide funds for children to go on school trips, and these concessions were particularly important. Andy had been working since he was 14 and paid for his own trips when he could; however, he found the concessions offered particularly helpful:

> "I think it was important to be able to go and not feel the pressure of having to save up the money, when you knew other people were getting their parents to pay." (Andy, 16 years, two-parent family)

> "If your mum can't afford a trip or dad, they pay half or you get money off or stuff like that. And then like my mum doesn't have to pay it by the deadlines, like she can pay it whenever she got the money." (Carrie, 15 years, lone-parent family)

Difficulties paying for school trips

Some low-income families can find even the deposit, or a reduced rate, hard to find:

> "I would have gone on this B... Adventure Centre and it was like £10 for the deposit, but mum didn't have the money and all the spaces went." (Nicole, 13 years, lone-parent family)

A few of the young people who were working were also paying for their own school trips; however, school trips were often costly, and, with clothes to buy and other social demands on their limited income, these young people were often making calculated decisions about whether to participate or not. For Nell it had meant that over the last couple of years she was not always able to go on the trips:

> "Sometimes I will pay for them or I won't go on the trip, it's quite simple. Because I will decide which ones are actually important to me and relevant to me, and if they are important then I will go on them and pay for them." (Nell, 17 years, two-parent family)

Not going on school trips

Half of the children in the study did not go on school trips with any regularity; some of these children were also not going on any holidays with their families (see Chapter Five for a discussion of children's opportunities to go on holiday). In these cases, a trip away with the school could have played an especially significant role in the children's social lives. One child had only ever been on one holiday and that was with his school. Cost was cited as a major cause of children missing out. Several of the more expensive trips involved children going to Germany or France to improve their language skills and to experience life in countries which they were studying. However, these children were also being excluded from the more general cheaper options:

> "I wanted to go to Germany and it was about a hundred odd quid and mum goes 'No'. It's like we go on a ferry, coach, really posh ferry, hotel, we get to meet friends there. And mum she said no. So I missed that.... I always miss out on the school trips and everything." (Bella, 12 years, lone-parent family)

> "There was like Alton Towers trips and things like that that I couldn't go on.... School trips were quite expensive, like we had this week at school where you could do different activities each day, and I'd end up doing like the free ones or the ones that didn't cost much 'cos everything else was too expensive." (Cherry, 17 years, lone-parent family)

When children did not go on school trips with their peers the social repercussions rippled far wider than the immediate impact of not sharing in the experiences of others on the day. School trips, particularly special occasions when children stay away, have a social excitement about them from the outset, and this can extend well past the actual event, enriched and informed by the retelling of memories and stories of the trip. Amy describes how she missed out on a special school trip and how she still feels uncomfortable and excluded from her friends' shared experiences of the trip:

> "Year 7 there was a French trip, it was one day and you stayed overnight on the ferry and most people went but I didn't go.... I don't know it was a lot of money for one day.... But even now my friends sometimes bring it up and I'm like 'Oh I didn't go, I can't talk about it'." (Amy, 15 years, two-parent family)

Alternative sources of income to help children from lone-parent families go on trips would seem to be absent parents; however, only one child talked about receiving any help from her absent mother to go on a trip:

> "When people are talking about it I feel quite 'Oh I wonder if dad's going to let me go...'. We went to London, that was the last trip we went to. That was the thing I was really worried because I knew within me that I really wanted to go, 'cos it was drama. It was going to see Miss Saigon and we also got to go to the Tate Gallery.... I wanted to go, and I knew I wanted to go and I was determined to go. So I was like well if dad says he can't then I'm going to write to my mum and ask her to send me the money." (Lisa, 15 years, two-parent family)

Schools generally provide a range of trips, some of which might be free or very cheap. However, having cheaper alternative options does not necessarily mean that children do not feel left out. For some children not going on trips also meant that they had to stay in school working, while their peers went away, and this was seen as particularly isolating and unfair.

Children who were excluding themselves

Of greatest concern must be the children who are excluding themselves from school trips. Several of the children in the study who were not going on any school trips indicated that they were very disillusioned with the process. In these cases children indicated that they felt there was no point even asking to go on trips so they didn't. In effect, these children were excluding themselves. Martin attended a large school where there were a lot of regular trips away and activities; here he talks about being resigned to not sharing in them:

> "I don't usually go on trips 'cos they are expensive and that.... At our school they do loads of activities and they go to loads of different places.... I don't bother asking." (Martin, 11 years, two-parent family)

Finding resources to participate effectively at school

Another area of difficulty mentioned by children and young people in the study was ensuring adequate resources for school to be able to participate fully. As we have seen, access to school uniforms was constrained; however, children and young people also highlighted difficulties obtaining books, stationery and bags for school, particularly in comparison with other children.

GCSE projects were also mentioned as an area where young people were struggling to sustain themselves, and where they felt having less money coming in was affecting them. School projects which are part of assessed course work caused particular difficulties, and young people were very aware of the need to keep up with others in the year, who would be examined alongside them. Amy had difficulty finding the money she needed for her textiles project, and then had to find more for an enterprise project:

> "Projects, it's just I got to do this business enterprise and you've got to make it as much as a business as you can.... I mean I was with a group, I put in my money and they weren't getting the stuff, so me and my friend split from them and we've done our own now. But I had to put in more money." (Amy, 15 years, two-parent family)

Brad had also had problems, and explained that he was especially aware of the differences between him and some of the other young people in his year. He had to find a suitable project to make for design technology GCSE, with a limited budget. This was something he would be marked on and given a final grade for, and he was afraid that he would be disadvantaged and his work viewed less favourably:

> "Like we're now doing this thing for my design technology GCSE, and you've got to design something and make it. And like there's people designing like things that will cost them like £300 and things like that, and mine cost £12.99 to build.... There's people building things for their cars that they'll get when they're 17, things like that. I'll be lucky if I get one by the time I'm 19 I expect." (Brad, 15 years, two-parent family)

As well as material resources, social costs were also evident, particularly where children were likely to arrange to do things as a group. Shared social activities at school, such as school discos and fêtes, can be particularly exposing for children who are trying to manage on a low income:

> "Like my friends are like saying are you doing this or are you doing that and I say no, 'cos I haven't got enough money or something like that. If they arrange to do something and I haven't got the money I say 'No I can't do it I ain't got enough money'." (Laura, 15 years, lone-parent family)

> "Well say I cancel like if they are sort of having a school fair there or something. My friends ... they are really good and they sort of like give me money and say 'There, go and get something with this'." (Sue, 11 years, lone-parent family)

Parents' views of school

Finding the resources to provide children with an adequate school uniform was also an area of concern highlighted by parents. Children were very clear in their interviews that having the right school uniform was particularly socially important. For parents the expense of providing the school uniform for their children was considerable, particularly for larger families:

> "It was very difficult to rig him out for the big school, that was horrendous.... I was lucky at the time because my dad helped me, without him I wouldn't have got through.... It was absolutely everything, I think I worked it out it was about £250 nearly £300. And that was you know blazer right down to black socks, shoes.... You can't let them go looking different, why should they?" (Izzie, lone parent)

Not all families are able to draw on a wider circle of kin for financial help, and schools are not always understanding about financial difficulties as far as uniforms are concerned (CAB, 2001). Della had tried to keep her son in school uniform but had also had ongoing arguments with the school when items of clothing wore out and she was unable to replace them:

"I agree that they should have a school uniform for the simple reason that they would want so many different clothes to wear, but it does annoy me when they outgrow their shoes and I send them to school with their trainers for a few weeks and then I get these letters saying your son is wearing trainers and I think yes I know, I will buy him some shoes when I can afford it." (Della, lone parent)

Interviews with parents about school trips revealed that this was an especially difficult area for those on a low income, particularly when trips were presented by the school as an important aid to their children's educational development. No one wants their children to be the ones who are left out, or to receive a less enriched educational experience than their peers. Parents like Annie and Jen were greatly concerned that their children would be left out or excluded:

"I get very annoyed when they come home and they say they want to go away on these school trips. I don't mind these day things that they go on and I don't mind like fundraising events. It's when they're going away for a week at a time and your child doesn't want to be the one left out and the one left at school." (Annie, lone parent)

"When they have school trips and things I have to say no and that's the hardest because we get so many letters home for school trips and with three it is a lot, the youngest one brought one home last week and it was for £100 and I just can't do it. I mean he understood because I think they know but it is still a lot of money." (Jen, lone parent)

Very few of the parents were able to send their children on any trips. One parent who had was Izzie. She had only one son still at home and was trying to ensure that her son could go on a school trip to France. She explained why she was determined that he should go if at all possible, even though at first she felt she could not afford it:

"I try and keep school trips going 'cos I don't see why he should miss out. He's got two coming up, but it is part of his schooling.... I mean ok it's a struggle to find the money but I will find it. Then he's got a trip to France coming up to a big park over there. First of all I said he couldn't go but then I thought no, 'cos he may never get the opportunity.... I will find it for him, I won't pull him out of it, 'cos he don't get a chance to go out a lot. I mean like the school said it's their first year learning French, it's a chance for them to have contact with French speaking people and to see it's slightly different to us. He's going on the tunnel, he may never get that chance." (Izzie, lone parent)

Schools do help, but previous research shows that parents are often unaware or uncertain about the concessions offered, and the implications of not paying a 'voluntary contribution' (Middleton et al, 1994). It was apparent from the parents' responses that not all of the families knew that they did not have to pay, or that there was help available to them. However, much depended on the approach of the individual school, and Annie's experiences revealed that even though parents may get help on one occasion there was no certainty that they will get it on another:

> "Unfortunately there's always a date by which this money has got to be paid in by and nine out of ten times it's not always dealt with so either the child has to go without completely or luckily sometimes you can come to an arrangement with the school, but it's not very often. I mean the first time it happened was with my eldest and I got help from the school, they've got like a fund that there's a set amount of money in that fund and if they chose to help then that's fine, but nine out of ten times they only do it that once.... Unfortunately I've got told this time around the school can't help you so I'm left to sort of try and pay a bit every week so she can go.... I don't see why my kids, just because I'm on benefit, why my kids should be the one that stays at home. At the end of the day that is not how it should be." (Annie, lone parent)

Noleen had children at two different schools and found that they had two very different approaches to helping:

> "The last time we had a concession with C... I think it was about 50 to 60 pence of about an £8.50 trip, it wasn't worth it. S... now he was very lucky, he's at the local comprehensive and he went on a trip to Exmoor and they paid for the whole trip and I was very grateful I really was.... We just go without food that week, usually 'cos I mean even just sort of eight pounds out of my money is days' meals, I'm not one of those mothers what can just sort of produce things out of thin air." (Noleen, lone parent)

It was also apparent that several parents knew that their children were self-excluding, and had come to accept this. In many ways, they felt that this was just as well as they could not afford to pay for the trips anyway:

> "They will tend to say I didn't want to go on that and manage to make quite a convincing case for not wanting to, and seeing as we couldn't have afforded it...." (Myra, two-parent family)

> "If it's silly things like it might be just a visit like the theatre or something we can't afford to do that. If it's both the kids going at the same time with the school or something we just can't afford to do it. But they [the children] seem to know what we can, they don't push it, they sort of say oh well, you know they know." (Tammy, two-parent family)

Parents' concerns about the cost of education

The cost of ensuring that their children are receiving an equitable education with their peers was a matter of considerable concern for parents on a low income. On top of the costs of providing a school uniform, and paying for school trips, parents are also increasingly asked for contributions towards their children's schooling (Middleton et al, 1997). For parents in the study these extra costs add worry and strain. As Tilly explained, even a seemingly reasonable sum, like £2, can strain an over-tight budget:

> "All the time they're bringing home something that wants money and even things they're doing in school wants money ... they did a medieval thing and you had to pay for that to cover food. Which obviously it's a contribution so you don't have to pay, but you have to give it to them otherwise he's singled out, see what I mean, then he's the one who feels awful. It might only be £2 but £2 is £2. Then there is cooking, he's started cooking now and that's ingredients every week." (Tilly, two-parent family)

For families like Jen's, where there were several children at school, the cost burden was even greater, and hard choices had to be made about priorities:

> "In sewing they had to have £2.50 for a cushion, I know it's not a lot but out of every week's money it is a lot, and then school photos, and then my middle one is making a box, like an ottoman box and he keeps, mum I need this, and it's costing me well up to now £30 just for wood and screws. So that week we have to have not a lot of shopping I'm afraid." (Jen, lone parent)

It was evident that increasing demands from schools were making some parents feel very frustrated and angry, and in some instances were creating tensions between children and their parents. In Hannah's case it was her children who had to explain to the school why she was unable to pay the full amount:

> "It's just that I can't pay that much. All right if it's a pound, two pound. But swimming they want like ten pounds. So all right maybe I try to give like two to three pound like a donation or something, but that's it. K... comes home and says 'mum they want to know why you've not paid a lot of money'. [I say] 'Tell 'em to sod off' sort of thing you know. They're forever asking for money at K's school for this that and the other." (Hannah, lone parent)

It was evident that the costs of adequate school participation were increasing and both children and their parents were aware of the pressures maintaining school appearances create. Solutions to some of these issues may lie in increased in-kind provision of goods and services in schools for children from low-income families. One of the few instances of this kind of provision was the free school meals service. In the final section of this chapter, we explore the role of free school meals in children's lives and how the children themselves feel about them.

Free school meals

The importance of the school meals service in providing an adequate and wholesome meal for children has recently gained the attention of policy makers, after a steady national decline in participation and service provision since the 1980s (Daniel and Ivatts, 1998). Nutritionally, free school meals have an important role to play in the health and development of children from low-income families[2]. However, previous research has indicated that free school meals are often viewed as problematic and as heavily stigmatised (Smith and Noble, 1995). Many of the children in the study felt that free school meals were a good thing, especially in schools where many other children were receiving them, where in effect the experience was a shared one. For some young people like Chris, who felt that they had to cut down on food at home, they were providing a welcome and adequate source of food:

> "We used to be able to eat like all the time really but not so much any more."
> (Chris, 15 years, lone-parent family)

Chris was happy with his free school meal; he was given £1.40 and allowed to choose whatever meals he wanted, like everyone else. Matt was also keen on free school meals; he said the thing that made him happiest was his dinner pass because it meant he got more dinners when he was hungry and needed extra at school.

However, for some children the issue of free school meals was problematic and several children from rural areas felt that free school meals made them very visible and more vulnerable to bullying. Nell explained why she did not have free school meals:

> "I don't because I realised when I was in Year 7 that the people who got free school meals were teased ... I couldn't handle that as I was already getting teased enough so I don't get free school meals." (Nell, 17 years, two-parent family)

Lisa had had to have free school meals, but she had always found them problematic until recently, when the system of tokens changed. Prior to this she was reduced to hiding her token every day, worrying that other children would see it:

> "At school it's difficult when I have to get a school token, like, to have my school meal 'cos, like, they pay for it, like, the benefits pay for it so it's just, like, 'Why do you get that?'. And then I have to explain 'Oh dad doesn't work' and it's like 'Oh!'... We used to have a paper token, which is little pieces of paper, and I'd go to the office and as soon as they'd give it to me I grab it in

my hand and screw it in my pocket. I do this every day, it's just habit really."
(Lisa, 15 years, two-parent family)

These children identify free school meals as a very specific and visible issue of difference, which clearly leads to fears of them being labelled and bullied. Stigma is one of the main reasons for low take-up of free school meals (Smith and Noble, 1995). However, the issue may not be the free school meal itself, as much as the process of qualification for it and delivery. The children who found it particularly difficult were children from rural areas, which may well reflect the more exposed position of poor children in rural schools, where free school meals are less common and consequently the children more conspicuous.

Parents' views on free school meal provision

Several parents talked about their fears of their children being stigmatised, especially where they themselves had painful memories of receiving free school meals as children.

Overall, however, the parents were happy with free school meals, and the most common area for concern was what happened in families during the holidays when free school meals were not available:

"The hardest part about free school meals is when they're off school you don't get that meal, and you've got to find more food, and you haven't really got the money. They're off for a couple of weeks now and it's gonna ..., I mean we 'aven't got much money as it is now, but we're gonna be so ... I mean free school meals is good 'cos they get a meal every day so you kind of use your money for shoes and stuff like that. But I mean when you get a couple of weeks like the last, six weeks during the summer holidays is terrible for us because we've got four of them at home, and all they want to do at that age is eat all day." (Jack, two-parent family)

"I miss those in the holidays 'cos we've got more to get and K... eats a lot, and they invite their friends in while you're down the shops and you come back and they've eaten a whole load of bread and you think 'Oh no'." (Jez, lone parent)

These accounts provide a different perspective on the value of free school meals. During the school term the provision of free school meals serves not only to ensure that children from low-income families have a nutritious meal, but also as a budgeting mechanism for parents. For these families the issue lies not with the free school meal as such, but with the lack of additional financial support for children during the school holidays, when there are extra mouths to feed.

Summary

Peer relationships play a critical role in children's lives in the development of self and social identity. Friendships and social relationships are valuable social assets, furthering social and material interests, providing support and enhancing social identity and social status (Allan, 1989). These values are reflected in the children's accounts of their friendships. However, friendships are rarely unproblematic, and the flipside of having friends and feeling socially included can be exclusion and bullying. Bullying was a significant issue for these children and nearly half of them had experienced bullying, either ongoing or in the recent past, and for some children it was sustained over a long duration. Their fears and their negative experiences of exclusion and bullying are apparent from their accounts.

Being able to wear adequate and suitable clothing also emerged as an important issue, and one that was identified by children themselves as socially significant. Their accounts reveal a high sensitivity to the nuances of fashion and the implications of being seen as not conforming to current fashion. Wearing the right clothes gave them the capability to sustain themselves within the clothing expectations of their peers and to avoid stigma, bullying and exclusion that could follow from 'inappropriate' clothing. However, the cost of getting the right clothes was prohibitive, and the children's accounts reveal some of the pressures they experienced in their endeavours to ensure that they were socially included.

By children's own accounts, schools are manifestly failing to provide them with a sufficiently inclusive social environment for their needs. They revealed school life to be fraught with the problems of bullying, material disadvantage and structural exclusion from shared activities through financial hardship. Half of these children were not going on school trips with their peers, some of them were self-excluding, feeling that the cost was too high even to approach their parents. As well as the dangers of exclusion from shared social activities, children were also keenly aware that material costs were affecting their school involvement, particularly during examination years when there were extra demands related to project costs and educational trips.

The last two chapters have used children's accounts to explore some of the material and social facets of children from low-income families' lives. Chapter Five looks at the personal and the familial. It reveals aspects of children's lives within their families, and explores children's own subjective understandings of the meaning and impact of poverty in their lives.

Notes

[1] Employers in the UK are increasingly stressing the importance of 'soft skills'. These are poorly defined at present but include personal qualities, friendliness, teamwork, communication skills, the ability to fit in and so on (Sparkes, 1999).

[2] The government is to reintroduce minimum nutritional standards for school meals in 2001 (Family Policy, 2000).

FIVE

Family life and self-reflection

The previous two chapters have looked at children's lives from both economic and social perspectives, and revealed the impact of poverty on each of these areas. This final chapter of qualitative findings focuses on children's home environment and their personal and familial lives. Children in general are rarely asked what their thoughts and feelings are, and the self-perceptions of children living in poverty are some of the most hidden. We have seen from the previous two chapters that inner worries, fears of social difference and stigma, and the impact of poverty on self-esteem, confidence and personal security may all exact a high price for children who are in the formative process of developing their self and social identities. Here is an opportunity to listen to children as they describe their own feelings, and the meanings they give to their experiences of poverty. They reveal their inner thoughts and fears, about their families, themselves and their futures. These are difficult areas for children to reflect on and during the interviews, when painful or difficult areas arose, great sensitivity was needed to ensure that the children felt free to pass on to other more lighthearted subjects. Sometimes this meant that children returned to these areas later, under the guise of other issues, as difficulties with friendships and worries about social acceptance can be particularly hard for children to articulate.

The chapter is in three main sections:

- Children's opportunities for play and leisure activities at home, how children use their free time and their capacity to join in shared clubs and other leisure activities with friends and peers in their neighbourhoods. Children's opportunities to experience some shared time with their parents and siblings away from home on family holidays are also addressed.
- Children's understandings and perceptions of money and need within their families. This section explores how children approach their own needs within the family, in the light of the potential conflict with their family's capacity to fulfil that need.
- Children and young people's perceptions of the impact of poverty on their lives. This section concludes with a look at what children would change in their lives if they were able to do so.

'Joining in': leisure time and clubs

We saw in the previous chapter that the children's opportunities for social interaction and shared social experiences are often severely constrained at school.

In this section, we focus on their opportunities for shared social activities with friends and peers at home.

Things to do at home

Children and young people in general tend to watch a lot of television and videos (Hendry et al, 1993), and, as expected, the majority of children and young people in the study talked about watching television, playing outside with their friends, and doing homework after school. Watching television was common, although not all children saw it as a choice; for some it was something to do in the absence of having anything else to do. Only four children out of the 40 talked about computers or play stations:

> "I watch the telly, that's all I ever do, I just sit and watch the telly, I don't ever go out." (Harry, 14 years, lone-parent family)

Time spent playing outside with friends was mentioned frequently, as was homework, as something the children did in the evenings. For young people with exams coming this was a necessity, but for other children homework was also a major part of the evening. Laura singled out homework as being particularly important for her, as she was anxious to succeed at school:

> "Stay in and just do course work, 'cause like it's my GCSEs, so I've got like loads of work to do and everything, so I hardly ever go out.... I just want to show people that I can do well." (Laura, 15 years, lone-parent family)

Weekends did not differ much; again the majority of children talked about watching television or playing outside with their friends. Few children from lone-parent families mentioned seeing their non-resident fathers.

Clubs and organised activities

In general, outside of the school environment, many children and young people enjoy a wealth of shared activities with their peers, through membership and engagement in youth clubs, after-school clubs, sports clubs and other organised activities. However, leisure time is becoming more commodified, and access to free or below-cost facilities has been severely reduced. Youth clubs and community discos are being replaced with private leisure centres, expensive sports complexes, bowling alleys, multi-screen cinema complexes and so on (Mizen et al, 1999). Participation and inclusion in this new leisure world is increasingly difficult for children from families with low incomes. Although the present government has shown a keen interest in improving the quality of youth services available to 13- to 19-year-olds, promoting a new vision for youth work in partnership with the ConneXions Service (DfEE, 2000, 2001a), the development of these enhanced services is still in its formative stage and the fieldwork areas of the study were characterised by a general dearth of affordable clubs and leisure facilities, with expenditure on young people in Somerset being particularly low (DfEE, 2001a).

Children and young people involved in clubs and leisure activities

Few of the children and young people in the study were attending clubs (these included youth clubs), and most of the children were not going to any sort of club or regular shared leisure activity with their peers. Those children that were attending clubs were very positive about them, and some of the children were also attending more than one club, particularly those that were keen on sports. Ray's involvement in clubs had meant more opportunities to meet friends and to share new experiences away from home. His comments were echoed by many of the children who were attending such clubs regularly:

> "You make new friends don't you, things like that. I've met a lot of friends through scouts, sailing and that." (Ray, 12 years, two-parent family)

The cost of participating

The opportunity to participate in regular shared activities and clubs was clearly valued by those that were able to do so. However, most of the children and young people in the study were not going to any clubs. Many of these felt that there was little on offer in their neighbourhood, and where there were clubs and other leisure facilities, the cost of accessing them was perceived to be a significant obstacle to joining and taking part. Costs fell into several areas: these included the cost of joining, or entry fees, and the extra costs of providing uniforms and equipment where they were required:

> "I'd like to go to tennis but I haven't got a tennis racquet, I want to get one but I can't." (Bella, 12 years, lone-parent family)

> "I like to go ice-skating and that more often but my mum can't afford it like all my other friends 'cos she ain't got as much money." (Mike, 12 years, two-parent family)

Children from rural areas appeared more likely to be attending clubs than children from urban areas, and they accounted for all the children attending youth clubs. This may be a result of the increased provision of mobile youth centres in Somerset, and a high attendance from children in villages where there were few, if any, other leisure options. For those children from rural areas who did have access to the mobile youth service, it was clearly highly valued, even though it often represented only a very small, and not particularly richly endowed, service. For children and young people from rural areas without access to the mobile youth service there was a complete dearth of leisure service provision.

Transport costs

Transport costs and accessibility also affect involvement with activities, particularly in rural areas (Davis and Ridge, 1997). Colleen had moved to a rural area from Birmingham, and found that it had considerably affected what she could do. Here she compared the transport costs:

> "I loved ice-skating, I used to go nearly every weekend and I can't do that now because it's in Bristol now. It's a bit of a fair way on the bus, you would have to pay at least £4 on the bus to go there, a taxi would be more. Yeah I do miss ice-skating. The pictures aren't that far but it was easier because the bus fares in Birmingham was only like 40p, and here its £2, so it's different." (Colleen, 13 years, lone-parent family)

In some of the study areas local facilities were particularly poor and there was little for children and young people to do. Involvement with clubs and organisations is associated with definite social benefits, including improved social skills, and the opportunity to meet and make new friends and social contacts (Erwin, 1993). Several of the children and young people identified clubs and activities as an opportunity to meet new friends, and this was borne out by the experiences of children who were attending clubs. Others like Carrie and Clarke were frustrated by their inability to meet more people and to do the things they wanted to do:

> "I want more places to hang around and meet more people but there's hardly anything." (Carrie, 15 years, lone-parent family)

> "I'd love to go somewhere mountain biking, but I can't get anywhere, you know. I ain't got no transport to do it, no money, I can't, I just can't do it." (Clarke, 15 years, lone-parent family)

Several children and young people did not even entertain the notion of attending clubs because they felt that the cost would be too high. These children and young people were no longer engaged in looking:

> "I don't really know, I haven't really looked into it. It's just the entry fee and that so I don't really go." (Nicole, 13 years, lone-parent family)

Children's and young people's experiences of their local neighbourhoods

Without access to transport, to move freely out of their immediate environment and to develop social networks and activities further afield, many of the children and young people were confined to their immediate locality. The quality and safety of the neighbourhood and the local community environment is an important consideration for such children (Greenfield et al, 2000). Some of the children and young people in the study were concerned about their neighbourhoods and felt generally unsafe or in some cases overlooked by hostile adults. Several children mentioned their fear of other children in their area and how this had affected their desire to venture out into their communities to attend clubs:

> "There is people I don't know and I just don't get along with them very well so I don't go ... I would like to go out more but there is too many weird people around so I can't." (Milly, 10 years, lone-parent family)

Children and young people from low-income families, living in rural areas, experienced very different neighbourhood environments to those children in urban areas. Children from urban areas were less secure in their neighbourhoods and more aware of the potential for violence and danger. Several children reported having moved from their previous houses because of drug taking and violence. Sal lived in an inner-city estate where there were frequent fights. Overall she felt that she coped with her situation but she was aware that sometimes circumstances got out of hand and she was then advised to stay clear of her usual haunts:

> "It's alright, it's friendly but sometimes it can get a bit out of hand.... The police just usually comes round and sorts everything out." (Sal, 12 years, lone-parent family)

Space to play in urban areas can be particularly difficult to find, and on the whole, children and young people indicated that what was available was often poor quality and restricted. Without a safe space for play, children tend to make greater use of their streets. However, children from low-income families are particularly at risk of being the victim of a road traffic accident (Quilgars, 2001). Previous research with children focusing on local neighbourhoods has found that traffic is seen by children themselves to be the greatest danger, far outweighing bullying, gangs, strangers and the fear of being attacked (Matthews and Limb, 2000). Cally had recently moved to a new estate in Bristol. She had felt very unsafe where she lived before, and she explained that a car had knocked her down when she was playing in the street. Although they had moved, she was still scared of the speed at which cars regularly went past her house where, in the absence of any other safe playing space, they were playing on the street:

"I was just playing by myself, like sort of on the edge of the road and I heard a car come speedin' round, so I just ... I was bouncing the ball and that so I moved out right close to the edge of the road edge, so I was like right close to it and then this bloke just come round the corner fast and knocked me over.... My ma came out and helped me anyway so to get me up and all that and I was covered in quite a bit of blood and that.... It's just like when the cars are coming off the main road like, like every two minutes, especially in the summer anyway when we are playing football or something." (Cally, 14 years, two-parent family)

Trying to find some space

In general children and young people like to make use of the streets and public spaces, and these play an important part in building cultural identities away from adult supervision and authority (Loader, 1996; Matthews and Limb, 2000). For teenagers the need for autonomous space is particularly important in their struggle to assert their independence. However, as Ennew (1994) points out, adult perceptions of adolescents are at best ambiguous, and while youth activities supervised by adults are called 'youth groups' and gain approval, unsupervised groups of youths are labelled 'gangs' and perceived as threatening (Ennew, 1994). Brad liked to hang out on the streets with a group of his friends at evenings and weekends, but he had experienced considerable harassment from adults in the past when they had been together:

"We used to get hassled down there, like, by older people, like men and that, used to come out and shout 'Get away from my 'ouse', like, 'cos they think we're going to break in and things like that. But none of us down there are like that. We used to get trouble with the police as well about drugs, 'cos there used to be one man down there he really didn't like us, he used to come out, chase us, threatening to beat us up like, and he'd already been in prison for GBH as well once." (Brad, 15 years, two-parent family)

Visibility and difference in rural communities

Although rural localities appear on the surface to be more desirable, children and young people from rural areas experience a different kind of neighbourhood pressure to their urban peers. This stems from the visibility and difference that accompanies the experience of poverty in rural communities which are predominantly affluent. As we have seen, children and young people from low-income families in rural areas have severely reduced opportunities for going beyond the confines of their rural communities. With nowhere to go, and nowhere to hide, they are correspondingly less able to escape from the adult gaze (Davis and Ridge, 1998). Several of the children and young people in the study were intensely aware of being excluded and felt powerless within their rural communities. Stewart lived in a small rural town; he felt frustrated and isolated, and was very aware of being overlooked:

> "Well I feel more safe in the house usually than when I am outside, 'cos when you're basically like on the other side of town and sometimes you feel like you're a bit unsafe, 'cos like the people might be watching you or something. Some people round here who like to watch in case you're doin' any trouble, you know sort of like neighbourhood watch sommat like that so you don't do sommat wrong. An' [even] if you do it right or something they might come out and say you're doing it wrong and call the police or something." (Stewart, 16 years, lone-parent family)

Matt and his family also lived in a picturesque rural village, but the small council estate he lived on was very isolated. He would have liked to have been able to go to a club but he was afraid to, because his brother, who had a learning disability, had been attacked and hit with stones on his way there, and the police had been called:

> "I wouldn't like to [go there] ... my brother's 18 and he went there last night, on the way to the club he got attacked.... So I don't really want to go to youth club ever, even when I'm 18." (Matt, 10 years, two-parent family)

In the same village, Kim, from a different family, was also having difficulties getting out and meeting people. She tended to mainly play at home on her own and was very isolated in her neighbourhood. She explained that she felt that her family did not fit in where they were living and that people were hostile and unfriendly towards them:

> "Well it's alright but people round, not like next door an' that but other people kind of don't like us round here, but we try and get along with them." (Kim, 11 years, lone-parent family)

What emerged from these children's accounts was a general dearth of opportunity for shared play and association. Their access to clubs and social activities was severely constrained by poor service provision, and where opportunities did exist, the cost of participating invariably restricted and reduced involvement. Without adequate transport and sufficient resources to participate in a wider range of social experiences, children and young people were effectively confined within their local environments. For many, these were characterised by insecurity, a lack of social space and in some cases, even hostility.

Parents' concerns about children's and young people's leisure opportunities

Parents were also concerned about the opportunities their children were having for shared social and leisure activities. Angela, a lone parent from a rural area, had great difficulty finding clubs or activities that her children could go to because of the lack of statutory provision such as youth clubs and the preponderance of costly uniformed activities, such as the cubs and guides:

> "There's always been a cost to anything they've done, whether it's been one pound a week or two pound a week, there's always been the extra, if they wanted to go away to camp, or they had subs to pay or membership fees, or you had to buy a uniform to go with that. There was always that extra cost.... If there was a youth club sort of thing you could have worn what you wanted to wear and it wouldn't matter who you were, you know they would have got on better, but as I say you can't have everything." (Angela, lone parent)

Trudy was also a parent from a rural area, and her children were only able to go occasionally to a small club that was run by a 'very religious group'. However, as she pointed out, she often did not have the petrol to take them there:

> "There's nowhere for them to go really, no matter where they play, they get moaned at.... F... Club on a Tuesday they go to sometimes, but it's down M... so it's taking and picking up and half the time you got no petrol so you say you can't go anyway." (Trudy, two-parent family)

Parents were as aware as their children of the quality of environment their children were experiencing. Tina's children lived on an urban estate where there were signs up saying 'No ball games', and this was a cause of hostility between the children and some of the adult neighbours. Tina pointed out that there was little else for the children to do, and the parks that were nearby were unsuitable for children to play in:

> "They all go out there playing football and then they get the police, and they moaned so much about it. And they never really done anything do you know what I mean, they were just kicking it around, people just got fed up of it. It's like when the police came I said there's nowhere for them to play, you give me somewhere for them to play then they can go off out.... You've got parks quite close, they're just up the hill, but it's all covered in dog mess and everything, anyway so. Not really there's nowhere for them what they can really go." (Tina, two-parent family)

Ian had moved into a rural area, and although his family were now having difficulties with transport, he explained that he felt that their previous neighbourhood was too violent for him to bring up his children safely:

"I moved because I wanted to get out of Y... because I didn't consider where I was living safe, as simple as that.... We had drug dealers living next door, and the police did nothing about it, 'cos they are unable to. It was a very sad situation. I mean there were gun incidents, robberies. Every car in our parking lot behind the flat had been broken into except mine.... You name it, it was happening there, knife fights the lot." (Ian, two-parent family)

Children's opportunities for family holidays

A shared family holiday is an event that has become particularly socially and culturally important in today's society; it is an accepted part of most children's and adults' lives. It provides an opportunity for families to relax together, to experience different environments and provides a break from their everyday existence. GPs believe holidays to be particularly important for families under any duress, particularly for the children (Family Policy, 2000). For children and young people in disadvantaged families, a break from the everyday struggle of managing on little money, and restricted social and leisure activities, may be especially important.

During the interviews the issue of whether children and young people were getting the opportunity to go away with their families for a short break or a holiday was explored. Half of the children and young people had not gone on any holidays in recent years, and in some cases had never gone on a holiday.

The value of holidays

Those children going on holiday had a younger age profile, with all of them except one being 13-years-old or under. It would appear that these children were less likely to get a holiday as they became older. Of those who did go on holiday, children in two-parent families who had a disabled parent or child in the family were in some cases able to tap into charitable societies that gave them access to holidays. Charitable societies are aware that holidays can have a particular importance for these children, particularly as they may have worries at home about a disabled parent or sibling. Amy's family used to have the use of a caravan by the sea, paid for by a charity. Here she talks about the value of those holidays for her:

"It's like a chance to get away and clear your head and everything. I like taking a friend 'cos mum and dad let us go off and do our own thing. You don't have to worry about school or about anything else at home, you could just get away from it all and have a good time." (Amy, 15 years, two-parent family)

Going on holiday was often a major undertaking for families, particularly financially, but also for families that had either no transport, or inadequate transport for their needs. Cally, who came from a large family, described travelling arrangements for a holiday that her family took at Butlins, where they had received help to have a holiday because of her brother's disability:

> "We sat there, all we was doing all day since half past seven in the morning is driving back and forward. We was living up in B... we drove from there to Minehead to back, to Minehead to back, all day. We started at half past seven and it got like to the place we was staying on the campsite at half past ten.... He picked my auntie up, took them down, he got her luggage and some others and my mum, and it's a pretty small car. Then he had to go back again, then he had to pick some more luggage up, and some of us lot up. Then go back down, pick some luggage up, go back down, then come back up and pick the rest of us, it was murder." (Cally, 14 years, two-parent family)

For some children in lone-parent families who were getting holidays, their mothers' boyfriends and/or non-resident parents played a key role in opportunities to go away on holiday. One child was going on holiday with his mother's boyfriend, and three children in lone-parent families were going on holiday with their non-resident fathers. Although one of these children was going on holiday with their mother as well, the others were not.

Children and young people who were not going on holiday

About half of the children and young people in the sample were not going on holiday with any regularity, and these ranged from children who had never had a holiday to children who had only sometimes been away. Access to affordable transport was again a factor, and over half of the children who were not going on holiday did not have any private form of transport. In lone-parent families, the change in circumstances brought about in some cases by parents separating, had signalled an end to holidays for some children, as the cost of spending time away became too much on a restricted budget. Some of these children talked about having been on holiday in the past, and their hopes that their non-resident parent might take them away some time in the future:

> "I haven't been on holiday for ages, I don't know how long ago. We've been a few places like when I was with my real dad, like abroad and things like that, but I haven't been anywhere for a long time." (Laura, 15 years, lone-parent family)

It cannot be assumed that children in the same family will have the same opportunities to go away on holiday either; there may be children from different fathers in one family and that may present different opportunities. Relationships can also be strained between non-resident parents and their children. Clarke lives with his mother and explained how he does not get a holiday when his siblings do because he does not like his father:

"We don't really go on holiday during the holidays. I usually stay at home. My little sister and brother go occasionally with my dad for a week or so. I don't normally go 'cos I don't really get on with my dad." (Clarke, 15 years, lone-parent family)

For children in two-parent families the onset of illness and disability, and the attendant extra costs associated with it, had sometimes meant that children could no longer go away on holiday:

"We used to go a lot before dad had real troubles with his neck, when he was still properly fully employed, and so we used to go about once a year to France. But since then, I mean at the moment after he has lost his job we haven't been on holiday as a family since then." (Andy, 16 years, two-parent family)

Some children like Adam had only been away on holiday very rarely in their lives, and yet the experience was especially valued and recalled with pleasure. Adam's father was disabled and he had only been away on holiday once in his life to stay in a caravan in Weymouth. It was a very exciting time for him and he wished he could go again:

"I got to go swimming and I got to go in a caravan, I never been in one.... My bed closed up to a wall.... There was like a little sort of wall and my bed was stuck to that bit there." (Adam, 10 years, two-parent family)

For those children who were not going on holiday, alternative means of getting a break such as school trips assume even greater importance. Lisa had never been away on holiday with her family, only with the school:

"I have only been with the school. I went to the Isle of Wight in the sixth, camping and stuff like that." (Lisa, 15 years, two-parent family)

For children who do not go on holiday the school holiday period can be particularly difficult; it can seem a long time particularly when other children go away for their holidays:

"It gets very boring towards the end of it, you just don't know what to do with yourself. You've got nothing to do and you don't know what to do." (Clarke, 15 years, lone-parent family)

The value of a holiday away, and a break from the immediate social and economic pressures that accompany disadvantage, was clearly evident in children's accounts. However, few of the children and young people in the study had experienced a shared holiday away from home with their families. For those children that did, the experience of having a holiday away was one they clearly valued.

However, for many of them, a holiday was a rare luxury, and for some, a luxury they have never experienced.

Parents' concerns about family holidays

Parents were also very aware of being unable to provide a family holiday away together. For parents like Jez and Jen it can be a particularly painful experience, when they were aware of their children feeling left out and different:

> "I don't think we've ever really been on a holiday.... I just couldn't afford it. With K... he does see his friends going off on these holidays with the school and so and so is going somewhere. I think he does sort of feel a bit left out like, but that's the way it goes, I keep telling him to do well at school so he can get a decent job." (Jez, lone parent)

> "We just couldn't afford to go on holiday, there's never any money left to save, it's just gone.... I would like to be able to say let's just go out for the day but I can't." (Jen, lone parent)

Some two-parent families had managed to get help from charities over the years to provide holidays for their families. However, the experiences of Myra and Dan indicate that relying on charities can have its own drawbacks. In Myra's case, there was only ever one holiday from the Mothers' Union, and although she had hoped they could have another it has not so far been forthcoming. In Dan's case, he felt that holidays were especially important for his children; they were very socially isolated and he feared that they were being picked on locally because of their poverty and because they were disabled. A holiday was one of the few social events they could enjoy. However, he had found the experience of fulfilling the bureaucratic requirements of the charities concerned daunting, particularly as he has poor literacy skills:

> "I just applied for a holiday for the children from the Family Fund, 'cos the children needed a break. So, I had a letter off them, off the fund to take to my doctor to fill out. Now I give it to my doctor, my doctor says 'Well I can't be bothered with all this, they'll have letters after letters, if they want me they can write to me' and I has to ring up the Family Fund to say 'the doctor says can you get in touch with him'. They say 'no it's not my place to get in touch with him, you've got to do that'.... I'm stuck in the middle." (Dan, two-parent family)

Children's perceptions of need satisfaction within their families

There has been very little research that looks at the social and economic understandings of children and young people from low-income families. What there has has been mainly quantitative (see Shropshire and Middleton, 1999), and suggests that children from low-income families are restricting their needs through their perceptions of their families' economic situation, arguing that these children are 'learning to be poor'. This could have a damaging impact on children's "immediate expectations and future aspirations" (Shropshire and Middleton, 1999, p 33).

This section of the interviews explored whether children from low-income families were restricting their needs within their families. It was also about children's thoughts and perceptions about what was possible for them. On being asked whether they felt that they would ask their parents if they wanted something which was quite expensive, nearly half of the children and young people said that they would, while just over half said that they would not even ask. The interviews went on to explore the responses in more depth, and looked with children at why they would not ask for something, and, for those that would ask, what they thought the outcome of asking would be.

Children and young people who would not ask for something expensive

Just over half of the sample would not ask their parents for something quite expensive, and within this group there was also a division between different perceptions of choice and in some ways autonomy. Many of them were children and young people who were either receiving pocket money or were working. These children felt that asking for something was not really an option for them as they had the capacity to harness their own resources and to save for anything that they felt they wanted; their responses were quite vibrant and positive. They said that they would not expect to be able to get something from their parents, but that they did have the capacity to get it for themselves and were quite prepared to do so. Colleen and Stewart described how they would manage:

> "Well I'd save up for it, if I wanted it that badly I'd save up for it. If I really, really wanted it I'd definitely save." (Colleen, 13 years, lone-parent family)

> "Save up for it, I got some money in the bank so I probably save up all my money for about as much as I could get, and if I could get it then I would probably get it when we went to that place next time." (Stewart, 16 years, lone-parent family)

For the remaining group of nine children, saving did not appear to be an option, and their responses were less positive and imbued in some cases with a sense of futility. These children and young people gave a variety of reasons why they would not ask their parents, and they tried to rationalise their inability to have things in different ways: by trying to forget about the things they wanted, by keeping quiet about it, by not even bothering to ask, and by trying not to care when they could not have things. Andy and Nigel felt that as there was little if any likelihood of them getting what they asked for, the best thing to do was to try and forget about wanting it:

"I won't really ask. I try to forget about it or something really." (Nigel, 10 years, two-parent family)

"I wouldn't I mean unless it was coming up to a birthday or Christmas I wouldn't ask really. I would just put it out of my mind." (Andy, 16 years, two-parent family)

Martin and Clarke were also realistic about their chances of getting something expensive that they wanted, and they indicated that they would not even bother to ask. In common with several of the children and young people, they showed a keen awareness that if finances were restricted, there was no point in putting pressure on their parent/s:

"I wouldn't bother, I don't see the point because if we haven't got very much money then we can't get it so I don't mind." (Martin, 11 years, two-parent family)

"Well I can't even bother if it's too expensive.... No is no, you know what I mean, I don't nag or nothin'." (Clarke, 15 years, lone-parent family)

Several of the older girls in particular were very protective of their parents, and were prepared to ration themselves and to go without in order that their parents were not worried by their demands:

"It's just impossible with four kids you know, if I get something then they will all want something so it's not really fair." (Lisa, 15 years, two-parent family)

"I knew it was a struggle for them, and I knew that what I wanted couldn't have been that important to go and ask for money and I just ... I've always got a sense when things are wrong and I can tell so I just won't ask 'cos I don't like asking for anything." (Amy, 15 years, two-parent family)

In this instance, they did not see themselves as antagonising their parents but rather that the experience of poverty was a shared one. We know from previous research that parents try hard to protect their children from the effects of poverty (Middleton et al, 1997). Here we see that many children and young people from low-income families were also engaged in trying to protect their parents. Laura's response sums up much of the sentiment expressed by the children:

> "It's not that she won't buy it for me it's like me asking for it. I just don't do it usually ... I don't like to do it 'cos like I know that she hasn't got much money and that, and all the bills she's got to pay and that I just don't like doing it. I would rather just go without instead of asking." (Laura, 15 years, lone-parent family)

Overall, these responses reveal not only children and young people's rationalisations, but also some of their understandings of their family's situation and the economic realities of their parents' lives.

Children and young people who would ask their parents for something expensive

Exploring the responses of those children and young people who would ask their parents reveals a very diverse set of expectations. Very few children felt certain that they would ask and be likely to get what they asked for, and of these most would only ask at birthdays and Christmas time. Some of the other children would ask relatives rather than their parents, but most of them indicated that even though they would ask, they were unlikely to get what they requested. Again, children in this group with regular pocket money or who were working responded that if they were unsuccessful in their request then they would then try to save their own money to buy what they wanted:

> "I would ask mum and if she hadn't got the money then I'd look an' see how much pocket money I'd got then I'd just save up." (Sue, 11 years, lone-parent family)

> "I would ask my mum and I would probably save up and wait over a period of time and then see how much I've got when I actually want to buy it." (Stevie, 12 years, two-parent family)

A few children and young people said that they would ask their parents to lend them the money to get something and then they would pay them back; most of these were working and negotiated help from their parents in a variety of ways:

> "Well if I had to get something straight away I would ask my parents if they could pay for it and I could pay them back." (Nell, 17 years, two-parent family)

> "I would see if my mum could lend me a bit of money and I would save up

the rest and pay her back that bit she lent me." (Kevin, 12 years, lone-parent family)

While at the outset there appeared to be very real differences between those children prepared to ask for something, and those who were not, further analysis shows that the differences between children were not as great as they initially appeared. Overall there were actually only four children in the sample who expressed any certainty that they would get something that was quite expensive if they asked their parents.

Self-reflection: what do children think about their life on benefits?

Children and young people were asked to reflect on their lives and to explore whether they felt that their families having less money and being on benefits had made a difference to their lives, and if so, how. This was a difficult area for children to focus on and explore, and in many ways exposed thoughts and feelings that children themselves may have been unwilling to acknowledge. Some of the children said that having less money coming in had made little or no difference to their lives. These were mostly boys and all but one were under 12 years of age. This may be an indication that as children grow older and spend more time outside their families in the company of their peers, the restrictions and social consequences of poverty may become more evident and important to them. However, although these younger children responded that having less money coming in had made no difference to their lives, their perceptions were frequently not borne out by their accounts which, in many instances, clearly showed the impact of having a low income. In some cases they were children in families where the other sibling interviewed saw the situation very differently. For example, a brother and sister in a two-parent family differed in their assessment of what impact having a low income had made on their lives. Jason was 10 years old and felt that being on benefits had made no difference to his life. His sister Sian was 16 years old, and felt that, although her family life had always been quiet and not much had changed, it was now becoming difficult for her to go out to see her friends, as her social life was increasingly located outside of her immediate home environment:

> "I mean I want to go out more now I'm getting older but it's hard when we haven't got a lot of money.... My friends get a bit pee'd off when I don't go in and see them, but it's not my fault." (Sian, 16 years, two-parent family)

The only child over the age of 12 who felt it had made no difference in her life was a 13-year-old girl who was the only 'only' child in the sample. She had consistently responded with a very positive outlook on life and had access to considerably more resources in terms of pocket money, holidays and so on than the others:

"Being like less money doesn't affect me at all. I'm still like the same person."
(Colleen, 13 years, lone-parent family)

Although it is clear that living on a low income had made a considerable difference to their lives, two of the older girls, living in two-parent families where there was a parent with a disability, also wanted to highlight the importance to them of having time with their families. Here Nell describes how she feels about living in a family on benefits:

"Oh it has made differences to our lives, like material things, we have hardly any of them.... But also because they are on benefits and my dad has got Disability Living Allowance he can't work, he's at home all the time and so we really have a lot more family involvement, and I think my relationship with my parents is a lot better than some of my friends." (Nell, 17 years, two-parent family)

The vast majority of the children and young people in the study felt that their poverty and their life on benefits was making a difference in their lives. They highlighted three main areas in which they particularly felt the impact of poverty: first, how their lives had changed since their families had been receiving benefits; second, how they felt poverty had affected their friendships and their opportunities to share in the same activities as their friends; and third, their fear of the social costs and repercussions of being seen to be poor and 'different'.

Many children and young people had experienced great upheavals in their lives which had coincided with their parent/s going on to benefits, either through disability or family break up. Carrie describes how it affected their family when her father left:

"When my dad used to live with us we was like, we wasn't really well off but we was just getting sorted, and we was able to have things we wanted. But when my mum had to go onto single parent benefit it was like a bit of a struggle. But we are coping now. There are some weeks when we haven't got much money, but some weeks it's like better. We take each day as it comes really." (Carrie, 14 years, lone-parent family)

Some children and young people like Laura had been living in families on benefits for a long time, and felt that they had always had to manage:

"I don't know what it's like not to be on benefits, so it's not as if like I haven't ever not been on benefits." (Laura, 15 years, lone-parent family)

For these children the impact of being on benefits was severe, and many found the restrictions difficult to bear, even though they were in some cases resigned to them:

"When we like want stuff we can't get it and we don't go out much." (Jack, 12 years, lone-parent family)

"Yeah it does make some differences 'cos like if I want something I have to save up for myself and like most other people that have got more money than me can ask their mums for more money and I can't ask my mum for that much money." (Kevin, 12 years, lone-parent family)

Missing out

One of the most important areas for children where they felt vulnerable from poverty was in relation to their friends and their opportunities to participate in the same things as their friends. We have seen in previous chapters how children and young people were experiencing great difficulty making and sustaining their friendships, and this was an area that was singled out as particularly problematic. The experience of social exclusion for these children was in part constituted by their inability to join in and to share in accepted social practices with their friends:

"I go out with my mum places, I don't usually go out with my friends.... If they arrange to do things and I haven't got the money I say no I can't do it, I ain't got enough money. Some of my friends are 'Oh I will pay for you', but I don't like to take their money either, so I say no don't worry I just won't come." (Laura, 15 years, lone-parent family)

"I would like to do more things with my friends, when they go out like down the town and that. But we can't always afford it. So I got to stay in and that and just in 'ere it's just boring, I can't do anything." (Mike, 12 years, two-parent family)

Missing out on shared occasions did not just mean shopping and leisure activities, but it also meant feeling excluded from the opportunity to meet up as a social group and to be included in group experiences. Brad and Martin highlighted some of the things they felt excluded from:

"They can go out on a night-time like. Go down town and buy themselves a load of new clothes and stuff like that." (Brad, 15 years, two-parent family)

"They go into town and go swimming and that, and they play football and they go off to other places and I can't go ... because some of them cost money and that." (Martin, 11 years, two-parent family)

Responses show some children and young people were resigned to doing less than their friends, and appear to accept the restrictions poverty placed on their social lives:

> "It's just that you can't have as much money as your friends and you can't do as much." (Charlene, 12 years, two-parent family)

> "If you can't do it you can't do it, you accept it don't you, you know. You just accept it really, you just carry on you know." (Clarke, 15 years, lone-parent family)

Several children clearly actively managed their social relationships to conceal their situation and to obscure their inability to participate. Hannah was rarely able to share in her friends' weekend activities and she felt this could make a difference to her relationships. So she got round this situation by putting on a show of indifference and saying that she just could not be bothered to go out. These were ways that children mediate their experiences and manage their relationships to save face and to cover up their inability to participate on equal terms.

> "See like on Fridays ... my friends have got lots of money and I haven't, if my dad can't afford it. So I don't really like to go places where they all go." (Hannah, 13 years, two-parent family)

Amy explains what she felt it was like when she was younger with her friends:

> "I did go out with them but it was sort of occasional.... Like when they went down town and they were spending their money, I'd go down town but not spend anything. If you're hanging around with people that are getting quite a lot of things from their parents and you are not, you feel you don't want them to know. That's the last thing you want them to know, and you're kind of like trying to keep it from them, and they're sort of like 'Oh why can't you go to the cinema' or summat. 'Oh I got some homework to do' or summat. You can't say." (Amy, 15 years, two-parent family)

Nicole also felt left out from her friends' activities and wished she had enough money to go out with them more. Unlike her friends, she was not looking forward to the Easter holidays and trips to the fair because she knew that she would not be able to get the resources to go. This meant that she was already dwelling on her exclusion from their company and worrying about her place in the group:

> "Just get out with my friends and do more stuff like um go into town. Like this Easter holiday like go to the fair and that. Where everybody else is going to be like, 'cos it's not just Sarah that's going and Lee and that, it's like my

friends from school. So I'll get a chance to see them and have a good time. But it's like the bus fare and the entry fee and then going on the rides and everything, so...." (Nicole, 13 years, lone-parent family)

It is evident from the children's responses that they have very clear thoughts about what they feel has been the impact of poverty on their lives. Although some of the younger children appeared unconcerned, overall the response from children was unequivocal; they were well aware of being poor, particularly in the company of their friends, and their responses reveal very real fears of social stigma and social exclusion.

Self-reflection: what children worry about

To develop a further understanding of the possible impact of poverty on children's self-identities and their inner thoughts and feelings, the interviews asked children what things they worried about in life. Almost a third of the children and young people in the study said that they did not really have any worries; the majority of these were boys. This was again a difficult area for self-reflection, and many of those who felt they did not have worries had previously indicated considerable concerns about their lives and well-being.

Those children who did talk about their worries were concerned about a range of things. These are children like any other children, and some of their responses reflected expected areas of concern. Several children mentioned being worried about bombing and war; a few were worried about bullying; and some of the girls were worried about getting boyfriends.

However, there was also an overriding concern regarding money, fear of failure, and debt, which would not be characteristic of children's general concerns. Overall their responses tended to fall into three categories:

* concerns about success or failure at school;
* worries about parents and money;
* concerns about the future.

Concerns about success or failure at school

The previous chapters have shown that children and young people have considerable concerns about their school lives; particularly regarding bullying, school trips and school uniforms. Children and young people in the study also expressed worries about success and failure at school, particularly about failing exams and not having done their homework. The school environment has become an increasingly intense experience for children, and those who underperform at school were at risk of exclusion and marginalisation. Harry was not doing well at school, and he worried a lot about his homework, although he was also resigned to getting into trouble because he had not done it:

> "[I worry] about my homework, if I'm going to get in trouble if I've done it wrong or something. But I don't really often do it so I'm not going to get it wrong I just get in trouble." (Harry, 14 years, lone-parent family)

Worries about parents and money

It was evident that many children were also worrying about their parents in ways that reflected the particular circumstances of their lives. For children in two-parent families, this often manifested itself as concern for their parents' health because of their disability. Children also worried about their parents' well-being and happiness:

> "When my parents are ill I worry about them a lot." (Jim, 10 years, two-parent family)

> "I worry about my mum a lot and I do worry that they can't always get everything they want and it makes me upset sometimes because they deserve it." (Amy, 15 years, two-parent family)

> "I worry about my mum and if she's like unhappy and stuff like that. Sometimes I worry about if we haven't got enough money, I worry about that." (Carrie, 15 years, lone-parent family)

For these and other children, worries about their parents' financial situation and their capacity to pay bills and to manage were also evident. Children and young people were very mindful of the financial situation in their families and often sought to protect their parents wherever possible. As well as money for their parents, several children said they were worried about getting enough money for their own needs and managing the money they had:

> "Not having enough money to go out with my friends, or not being able to have, like, as much good stuff as they've got." (Charlene, 12 years, two-parent family)

> "You can't do as much and I don't like my clothes and that. So I don't really get to do much or do stuff like my friends are doing.... I'm worried about what people think of me, like they think I'm sad or something." (Nicole, 13 years, lone-parent family)

Concerns about the future

Some of the children talked about being very afraid for their futures, and showed great insecurity about what their futures may be like:

> "I worry about what life is going to be like when I'm older.... Because I'm kind of scared of growing older but if you know what's in front of you it's a bit better, but I don't know." (Kim, 11 years, lone-parent family)

> "I don't know sort of like the future what's going to happen and that. I might not get a good enough job and all that." (Cally, 14 years, two-parent family)

Bella was already very isolated at home and having difficulties maintaining her friendships and taking part in shared group activities. Here she talks about being afraid that she does not fit in or wear the right clothes, and her fears for the future:

> "I don't fit into groups. I'm weird. I like wear clothes that don't suit. Sometimes I dress up, but I don't know what to wear. I worry about when I get old and I die. I just basically burst into tears. I just don't want to die when I'm older. It makes me worry would I ever fit into a group or would I ever have children." (Bella, 12 years, lone-parent family)

Parents' reflections on the impact of poverty on their children's lives

The parents, like the children, were asked to reflect on their lives and whether they felt being on benefits had made a difference to their children's lives. Several parents like Dan felt that their lives had changed, not just through having less money but also in their relationships with others. Dan explained:

> "Life on the social is a life of charity, you get to act like a charity. I know it sounds horrible and I don't like being a charity but I've got no other choice." (Dan, two-parent family)

Tilly and Jack sum up the feelings of many of the parents; they know their children were going without things that most other children have, but they felt powerless to do anything about it:

> "They know that mum hasn't got the money, I'll say to them oh mum can't afford oh this that and the other. But they don't keep on, if I haven't got it then they know that we can't have it." (Tilly, lone parent)

"The thing about benefits is yeah, you can live on 'em but it's always the kids that suffer at the end of the day isn't it." (Jack, two-parent family)

Self-reflection: what children and young people would change

Towards the end of the interviews children were asked what would make a difference in their lives, or what they would do if they had a magic wand and could change anything they liked. Not all the children were able to think of things that they would change, but those that did said that they would change a range of things. Surprisingly only a few children mentioned using a wand to create actual things like a television or a bike. Many of the children's responses reflected their realities of their environments. Some of the children who were living in an overcrowded house wanted to move house or to change their space.

Several children in families where a child or parent had a disability wished that they could bring about some changes in the life of that person. One girl wanted her brother who had Attention Deficit Hyperactivity Disorder (ADHD) to be a nicer person and another girl just wanted her father to get better, and felt that the difference it would make in her life would be not just financial, but also social:

> "Make my dad better so he could go back to work. I'd have more money coming in, it would make him not so protective over me as well, 'cos he can be over protective and doesn't let me go out." (Sian, 16 years, two-parent family)

Several children and young people wanted to change things so that they could see more of their friends or be more social. These changes very much reflected the responses children had given earlier about the difficulties of meeting up with friends, going on holiday and having the space for leisure activities:

> "If I could change something I would do something like bring a beach closer kind of thing so we could get out more." (Peter, 12 years, lone-parent family)

> "If I could change something I would probably change where I live because like none of my friends live round here." (Charlene, 12 years, two-parent family)

> "To have like something to do around the village.... Like putting in a few places where we could go, parks that are more advanced for our age." (Shamus, 12 years, lone-parent family)

Many children and young people in the sample talked about how having more money would make a difference to their lives. Surprisingly only one child mentioned winning the lottery, and one girl just wanted her mother to have more money for herself. Brad was concerned for his future and wanted to change things so that his children would not be poor. Lisa wanted more money so that she could go to the shops with confidence and feel that she could buy things if she wanted them:

> "To have more money that's all, go to college so I can get a job so my kids don't have to go through it like." (Brad, 15 years, two-parent family)

> "Because I would be able to get things myself. I don't know, I feel like there is something in me waiting to come out when I've got the money to do it.... For instance shopping, when I am trying on stuff you know, I can try it on and say I'm going to take this home." (Lisa, 15 years, two-parent family)

The final words are left with Amy, who identified some of the ambiguities that children revealed when they reflected on their lives and the things they would change. Amy had experienced great upheaval in her life due to the onset of her mother's severe disabling illness. She was aware that she had lost much but she was also an active and enquiring young person who was engaged in making sense of her experiences and taking control of her situation where she could. She was grateful for the support that benefits provide for her family, but was also acutely aware of the difference and disadvantage that they bring:

> "If I could go back and change what happened then I would but I don't know, I don't regret being on benefits 'cos it's made me learn, it's made my brother learn, my mum and dad, and it's helped. But I think that sometimes you wish you could have things for your family that other families have got." (Amy, 15 years, two-parent family)

Summary

This chapter has focused on children's lives at home and in their neighbourhoods. Beyond the school environment, we have seen that children's social and leisure time has been characterised by poor engagement of children in the little provision that was available to them. Children's accounts reveal a poverty of opportunity, with transport and participation costs impacting on their capacity to participate in shared organised activities with their peers. It was not that these children and young people did not wish to join in, rather that they were unable to do so. Entry fees, uniform or equipment costs and transport availability and cost have all been cited as barriers to participation. Children's and young people's experiences of their neighbourhoods revealed concerns about safety and traffic for those living in urban areas, and worries about increased visibility and stigma for those living in rural areas.

On the issue of holidays, it was apparent from children's and young people's accounts that when they did get the opportunity to go away on holiday the experience was a particularly precious one. For those from lone-parent families, the provision of holidays and treats away were an area where non-resident parents appeared to provide some benefits in kind. For several children and young people these were the only possibilities of experiencing holidays, but this was not a holiday with the parent with care, generally the mother, but rather a holiday with the non-resident parent only. For two-parent families, the presence of a disabled adult or child within the family meant that access to holidays could be facilitated by drawing on charitable support as a resource. However, as the parental responses indicated, relying on charity was not necessarily a secure or comfortable option for families. Many of the children in the sample had not had a holiday for some time; in some cases the children had never had a holiday away with their families. For them the impact was felt not just in the lack of a holiday itself, but also by social comparison with their peers, who were able to go away during school holidays. This engenders feelings of difference and of being left behind.

The second section of this chapter focused on children's and young people's perceptions of their family's capacity to respond to their needs. It examined what children and young people felt was possible in the light of the economic constraints operating within their families. To explore this issue children were asked what they would do if they wanted something and if it was quite expensive, would they ask their parents and would they expect to get it? Although there appeared to be considerable differences between those that would ask, and those that would not, when children discussed their understanding of the likelihood of getting what they had asked for, a far more complex picture emerged. It was apparent that even when children would ask for something, there was little expectation that they would receive it. Only four children out of the sample of 40 expressed any certainty that they would get what they had asked for. The remainder all felt they would either be refused, would need to borrow or save their own money, or, in the case of half of the sample, that asking itself was not even an option. Children and young people also showed a considerable awareness of their parents' financial situations, and there were signs that some of them were trying to protect their parents from the impact of poverty, in some cases through a denial of their own needs and aspirations.

When children were asked to reflect on their lives on benefits, it was evident that these were children who were well aware of the impact of poverty on their lives. For many children the advent of poverty had accompanied severe upheaval in their lives, through family illness and disability, or family breakdown. For others, a life on benefits was all they had ever known. The effect of poverty on their social involvement and their friendships was an area particularly highlighted by children. Fears of social detachment and social difference were expressed, and children were especially aware of being excluded from the events and activities of their friends and social groups. When children talked further about their worries, their responses revealed a set of very adult issues. Fears and concerns for parents were evident, and reflected an element of family insecurity. Children were also worried about money; about how their parents would pay bills; and about whether there would be enough for their needs, as well as their family's. There were also signs that for some children financial and social insecurity in the present was being reflected in fears and uncertainty for the future.

Finally, given the imaginary opportunity to change anything at all about their lives, we find that, remarkably, children did not have an instant wish list of expensive toys and possessions. For most of them, the things they would change were related to the mundane everyday struggles in their lives: the need to have more space, or a break from the worry of a disabled family member, or more opportunities to be social and to see friends. Above all, children wished for more money to ensure some measure of security, not just for themselves, but so that their children would not have to experience what they were experiencing now.

SIX

Experiences and perceptions of school: analysis of the BHPYS data

The three previous chapters focused on qualitative data, which explored how children and young people from low-income families see their home and school lives, and their social and familial relationships. This chapter seeks to build on that knowledge and to develop a wider understanding of children's and young people's lives through a comparative analysis of large-scale survey data. This provides an opportunity to explore the differences between children and young people who are living in low-income families with those who are living in families with adequate incomes. The chapter is based on analysis of data from the 1997 British Household Panel Youth Survey (BHPYS)[1]. The data is used to explore children's experiences and perceptions of school life. Throughout the chapter the analysis is underpinned by a key question:

• Do children in the Survey, who are living in households in receipt of means-tested benefits[2], differ from children living in households that do not receive benefits, in their experiences and perceptions of school life?

An essential part of children's and young people's lives is spent in the school environment, and the importance of disadvantaged children's academic performance for their future well-being and employment prospects is considerable (Gregg et al, 1999). However, as we have seen from the qualitative study, children's perceptions of school life and their everyday experiences of school life are also an integral part of developing an equitable and inclusive academic environment. The current Labour government has made a strong policy commitment to improving the educational prospects of disadvantaged children (DfEE, 1997), and policies have been put in place to tackle a range of issues, including literacy, numeracy, truancy and school exclusions (DSS, 1999a). We have seen from the qualitative study that children from low-income families have particular concerns about the quality of school life they are experiencing, and their opportunities to 'fit in' and join in with the opportunities available to their peers at school. In this chapter we will draw on a large sample of children and young people to develop a comparative insight into a range of school issues, including children's experiences of school, their perceptions of their teachers and the role their parents play in their academic lives.

Although it is desirable to broaden and enhance findings emerging from qualitative research, finding child-centred large-scale survey data is problematic. Perhaps even more so than in qualitative research, children's views and experiences have been largely ignored in large-scale surveys. Children have rarely been the focus of such surveys; in fact, children have rarely even been seen as fully functioning members of households. As Scott et al (1995) argue, they are at worst ignored and at best treated as auxiliary members. The acknowledgement that children could have views of their own, and their own perceptions and experiences to recount, has often been missing. However, as issues relating to children have become more centre stage, so, too, has their gradual inclusion into statistical data. The BHPYS (started in 1994) is an extension to the ongoing BHPS and does collect data from children[3].

A total of 720 children and young people responded to the youth questionnaire in 1997. Their ages ranged from 11 to 15 years[4], 53% of the sample were boys and 47% were girls. Table 6.1 shows the number of children in the sample who were living in families on Income Support/Jobseeker's Allowance (IS/JSA). Unlike the children living in families receiving Income Support interviewed in the qualitative study, this sample is made up of two groups of children, those living in Income Support households and those living in households where the parent/s is unemployed and receiving Jobseeker's Allowance[5]. The total number of IS/JSA (benefit)[6] children in the sample was 112, representing 16% of the sample. This is a lower percentage than in the general population, where 20% of all children (under 16 years old in 1997) were living in families that received IS and JSA (DSS, 1998).

Throughout the analysis a range of variables were used to establish the influence of other factors on children's responses. These included family type, age, gender and work status. When these factors have proved significant they are highlighted in the text. Where appropriate, analysis using a small sample of Family Credit children was also carried out to explore the differences between benefit children, Family Credit children and others. However, this is a very small sample (45 cases), and the findings are not sufficiently robust to report with any certainty. Nevertheless, the opportunity to explore the responses of a group of children and young people who were living in households receiving Family Credit is still a valid exercise, particularly in the light of the government's renewed commitment to encouraging parents into work and to providing in-work support for low earners through Working Families' Tax Credit.

In this chapter we focus on the experiences of school life for children from low-income families. School was also an area of importance highlighted by children in the qualitative interviews; therefore, this additional data and analysis

Table 6.1: Number and percentage of children in IS/JSA sample

	Number of children	Sample (%)
IS/JSA	112	16
Non-IS/JSA	608	84
Total sample	720	100

Source: Author's analysis of BHPYS (1997, Wave 7)

will help to contribute to our overall knowledge and understanding. The chapter starts by exploring children's and young people's experiences of school (suspensions and expulsions, truanting and bullying), and then considers their relationships with teachers, and finally, their perceptions of school as a medium of success, and of self and parental involvement.

Children's and young people's experiences of school

During the 1990s school exclusions significantly rose, and there are over 11,500 permanent exclusions from secondary schools every year (SEU, 1998c). The issue of school exclusions and truancy were prominent on the new Labour government's agenda and these were some of the first issues addressed by the Social Exclusion Unit in 1998 (SEU, 1998c). The intention in this chapter is to develop a holistic understanding of children's and young people's experience of school, and their perceptions of school in childhood.

Suspensions and expulsions

This first section of analysis explores children's self-reporting of exclusions and expulsions from school. Although we have official data relating to fixed and formal school exclusions, there is no official data relating to children and young people who are excluded informally. Children's own accounts of being excluded may reveal something of everyday school practices and how they impact on children and young people themselves. Table 6.2 shows that overall only 4% of children in the sample reported being expelled or suspended from school, and this is as expected, as the number of permanent school exclusions in the general school population is very small compared to the overall school population (SEU, 1998c). However, the incidence reported by benefit children is significantly greater than that reported by children in the rest of the sample. Nine per cent of children in benefit households say that they have been expelled or suspended from school in the last year compared with only 3% of children in non-benefit households.

However, it may be that children and young people who have been suspended or expelled are different from other children in some respects, so to examine the possibility of other underlying factors, the effects of other factors were explored. The age of the child did emerge as significant in both the benefit and non-benefit samples. As children became older, they were more at risk of being suspended or expelled than when they were younger. Table 6.2 shows that teenagers (6%) were significantly more likely to report being suspended or expelled than pre-teenagers (1%). However, in the benefit sample there was a much larger difference between pre-teenagers and teens, with 14% of teenagers in the benefit sample reporting being suspended or expelled compared to only 2% of pre-teenage benefit children. Furthermore, very few of the non-benefit teenagers reported being suspended or expelled.

The influence of gender was also apparent. Table 6.2 shows that boys (6%)

Table 6.2: Children and young people who have been expelled or suspended from school in the previous year, by benefit receipt, age and gender (%)

	Benefit[a]		Non-benefit		All	
Suspended/expelled						
Yes	9		3		4	
No	91		97		96	
Base (100%)	(114)		(606)		(720)	
Age group	Pre-teen	Teen	Pre-teen	Teen	Pre-teen	Teen
Suspended/expelled						
Yes	2	14	1	4	1	6
No	98	86	99	96	99	94
Base (100%)	(49)	(65)	(229)	(377)	(278)	(442)
Gender	Boys	Girls	Boys	Girls	Boys	Girls
Suspended/expelled						
Yes	14	3	4	2	6	2
No	86	97	96	98	94	98
Base (100%)	(61)	(53)	(309)	(297)	(370)	(350)

[a] In this and all subsequent tables IS/JSA children will be called benefit children.

Source: Author's own analysis of BHPYS (1997, Wave 7)

were more likely than girls (2%) to report being suspended or expelled. Benefit boys were significantly more likely to report being suspended or expelled (14%) than non-benefit boys (4%). However, the difference was not significant for girls. While age and gender were significant factors in suspension and expulsion across the whole sample, benefit children were still more likely to report being suspended or expelled than non-benefit children.

To explore these relationships further, and to explore some of the factors influencing which children were most likely to report having been expelled or suspended from school, a LOGIT model was run[7]. An additional sub-sample of children and young people living in families in receipt of Family Credit was also identified and entered into the model. Table 6.3 shows that (as predicted), gender is a significant factor in whether children reported being expelled or suspended from school. The odds of boys reporting being suspended or expelled were three times greater than those for girls. Age is also a factor for all children, and the odds of teenagers reporting suspensions or expulsions were three times as great as those for pre-teen children. Whether children and young people were working or not was not a significant factor. When we look at children living in families in receipt of benefits, an interesting picture emerges. As expected from earlier analysis, benefit children are three times more likely than children not on benefits to report being suspended or expelled, and those most at risk were teenage boys living in a household which receives either benefit or Family Credit. It is interesting to note that children living in families in receipt

Table 6.3: Odds of children and young people reporting being suspended or expelled from school in previous year

Characteristics	Odds ratio for suspensions/expulsions
Girls	1.000
Boys	3.219**
Pre-teenage	1.000
Teenage	3.324*
Children not working	1.000
Children working	1.499
Non-benefit	1.000
Benefit	2.933*
Family Credit	4.723**

Notes: 1.000 indicates reference category. Odds for reference category = 0.005.

* Significance at P<0.05, **significance at P<0.01.

The reference category is a girl, she is a pre-teenager, not working and living in a household that is not in receipt of either Family Credit or benefit. Her chances of being suspended or expelled are very low (see odds above). For brevity, when a child is referred to as having particular characteristics the author only refers to the characteristics that are different from the constant.

Source: Author's own analysis of BHPYS (1997, Wave 7)

of Family Credit were the most likely to report suspensions or expulsions. Teenage boys in such families were nearly five times as likely as teenage boys in non-benefit families to report being suspended or expelled from school.

Truanting

Although whether a child has been expelled or suspended may reflect the quality of relationships that the child has within their school environment, truanting is also an indication of a child's willingness to be present or absent, to engage or to withdraw. Truancy rates in the overall school population are hard to establish; official figures show relatively low rates, but surveys of young people show the rates to be much higher (SEU, 1998c). The Social Exclusion Unit report suggests that at least one million children (15% of all pupils) take time off from school without permission (SEU, 1998c). This section explores children's responses to a question about the frequency with which they truanted from school. Of all children, only 10% reported that they truanted once or twice and 5% more frequently. However, benefit children were significantly more likely to truant frequently than others.

Table 6.4 shows that 11% of children in benefit households truanted frequently from school compared with 4% of children in non-benefit households. Within the benefit sample, there were no significant differences in the rates of truancy by gender, family type or the number of children in the household. The only significant factor was age; older children were more likely to truant than younger

Table 6.4: Children truanting from school, by benefit receipt (%)

	Benefit	Non-benefit	All
Truanting from school			
Never	80	85	85
Once or twice	9	11	10
Frequently	11	4	5
Base (100%)	(114)	(606)	(720)

Source: Author's own analysis of BHPYS (1997, Wave 7)

children, teenagers more likely than pre-teenagers. This reflects findings from the Social Exclusion Unit report, which showed that truants tended to be older pupils from poorer backgrounds (SEU, 1998c).

A LOGIT model (Table 6.5) shows the odds of a child or young person truanting; as expected, being a teenager is a significant factor for all of the children. The odds of a teenage child truanting were three times greater than those for a pre-teenage child in similar circumstances. Of particular interest is the effect of whether or not a young person is working. Children and young people working were nearly twice as likely as non-working children and young people to truant. Benefit receipt is also a major factor underlying whether or not children truant. Children in a benefit family were nearly twice as likely as children in families not receiving benefits to truant. However, as for suspension and expulsions, living in a household receiving Family Credit is the most significant factor. The odds of children from families in receipt of Family Credit truanting were more than three times as great as the reference category and nearly twice as great as benefit children.

Table 6.5: The odds of children truanting

Characteristics	Odds ratio for truanting
Pre-teenage (11-12)	*1.000*
Teenage (13-15)	3.383***
Children not in work	*1.000*
Children working	1.716**
Non-benefit	*1.000*
Benefit	1.920**
Family Credit	3.584***

Notes: 1.000 indicates reference category. Odds for reference category = 0.049.

* Significant at P<0.10, ** significant at P<0.05, *** significant at P<0.01.

The reference category is a pre-teenage child, who is not working, and lives in a family that receives neither benefit or Family Credit. For brevity, when a child is referred to as having particular characteristics, the author only refers to the characteristics that are different from the constant. The odds of them truanting are very low (see odds above).

Source: Author's own analysis of BHPYS (1997, Wave 7)

Bullying

Children experience school as a medium for learning and achievement, but also as an important social environment. As we have seen from children's qualitative interviews, maintaining adequate and rewarding social relationships at school are a major concern for children. One aspect of school life as a site of social relationships is the fear and actuality of being bullied. Children and young people who are bullied have difficulties concentrating on their schoolwork, and often experience increased rates of absenteeism; they are also more likely to be depressed, anxious and to suffer from low self-esteem (Sharp, 1995; Hawker and Boulton, 2000). The qualitative data showed that the benefit children and young people interviewed were experiencing a high degree of actual bullying at school. Here we explore how much benefit children worry about being bullied at school in comparison to their peers.

Table 6.6 shows that overall a third of all children in the sample (33%) were worried to a greater or lesser extent ('a bit' or 'a lot') about bullying at school. However, when we look at the benefit children they were significantly more likely to worry 'a lot' about being bullied (11%) than non-benefit children (4%). The differences between benefit children and non-benefit children appear most marked at the extremes of being worried, as they were when looking at truanting. There is little apparent difference between the two groups when worrying 'a bit' about bullying.

Exploration of other factors that might influence whether or not children worried about bullying found that there was no significant effect according to age. Gender was a significant factor, but this time it was benefit girls who were particularly concerned about bullying. Table 6.6 shows both benefit girls and non-benefit girls were significantly more likely than their male counterparts to

Table 6.6: Children worried about bullying, by benefit receipt and gender (%)

	Benefit		Non-benefit		All	
Worried about bullying						
Not at all	64		68		67	
A bit	25		28		28	
A lot	11		4		5	
Base (100%)	(114)		(606)		(720)	
Gender	Boys	Girls	Boys	Girls	Boys	Girls
Not at all	77	48	77	58	77	57
A bit	15	38	22	35	21	35
A lot	8	14	1	7	2	8
Base (100%)	(61)	(53)	(309)	(297)	(370)	(350)

Source: Author's own analysis of BHPYS (1997, Wave 7)

worry about bullying at school. Overall, over half of the sample of benefit girls (52%) were worried to a greater or lesser degree about bullying. It may be that those children who report worrying about bullying 'a lot' are those that have also experienced the most bullying. Benefit girls were more likely to worry 'a lot' about bullying than non-benefit girls (14% and 7% respectively). Therefore, the area for the most concern may well be those children and young people who are worrying 'a lot' about bullying as this may be having an effect on their security and confidence at school.

Table 6.7 shows that, as expected, the odds for girls worrying about bullying 'a lot' are three times greater than those of boys. Both benefit and Family Credit categories show greater odds of worrying than do the reference category of no benefits. However, only the benefit category shows a significant difference. The odds of a boy on benefits worrying about bullying 'a lot' were three times greater than those of a boy who is in a non-benefit household. Girls on benefits were the group most likely to worry a lot about bullying; they were 12 times as likely to worry about bullying 'a lot' than the reference category. They were also three times as likely to worry as girls who are in non-benefit families.

Thus, when we look at children's experiences at school, some clear differences have emerged between benefit children and other children in the sample. In each area of enquiry, children and young people living in families in receipt of benefit gave significantly different responses to those given by non-benefit children and young people. They were more likely to be suspended and expelled, play truant and be fearful of being bullied. These responses were also mediated through factors of age and gender. Teenage boys in benefit families are more likely than other boys to say that they have been expelled or suspended from school. Teenagers in benefit families also report higher rates of truancy than non-benefit children, and girls in benefit families were significantly more likely to worry 'a lot' about bullying than other children, with over half of the benefit sample of girls expressing concern about bullying. When the sub-group of children in households receiving Family Credit are included in the analysis,

Table 6.7: Odds of children worrying about bullying 'a lot'

Characteristics	Odds ratio for worrying about bullying a lot
Boys	*1.000*
Girls	3.609*
Non-benefit	*1.000*
Benefit	3.384*
Family Credit	1.993

Notes: *1.000* indicates reference category. Odds for reference category = 0.0169.

* Significant at P<0.01.

The reference category is a boy living in a family that receives neither benefits nor Family Credit. The odds are very low that this child will worry about bullying 'a lot' (see odds above).

Source: Author's own analysis of BHPYS (1997, Wave 7)

they also show similar patterns to the benefit sample; being in a household in receipt of Family Credit raises the odds significantly for being suspended or expelled. They were also significantly more likely to say that they were truanting from school than other children.

Children's relationships with their teachers

The second section of the analysis explores children's responses to questions about their relationships with their teachers, a critical area for understanding how children engage with learning.

Do children and young people like their teachers?

First, children and young people were asked whether they liked most of their teachers. As Table 6.8 shows, the majority of children, over 70%, agreed that they did like most of their teachers. There were no significant differences between benefit children and non-benefit children.

Do children feel that their teachers are always 'getting at' them?

Although it would appear that overall most children liked their teachers, this response may represent children's desire to like most of their teachers. The realities of their relationships with their teachers may differ, however, and this was explored in the next two questions, which focus on whether they feel that their teachers like them. Cox (2000) suggests that teachers' attitudes and behaviours towards their pupils can have a powerful influence on children's academic motivation and progress. Studies with young people show that they have strong notions about what constitutes a good teacher, and a common complaint is about teachers who are perceived to be 'unfair' (Ruddock et al,

Table 6.8: Whether children like their teachers or not, by benefit receipt (%)

	Benefit	Non-benefit	All
I like most of my teachers			
Strongly agree	17	15	15
Agree	54	59	58
Disagree	21	18	19
Strongly disagree	8	8	8
Base (100%)	(114)	(606)	(720)

Source: Author's own analysis of BHPYS (1997, Wave 7)

1996; Cox, 2000). Young people were asked whether they felt that teachers were always 'getting at' them.

As can be seen from Table 6.9, overall 21% of children said that they felt that their teachers were 'getting at' them; however, benefit children (28%) were significantly more likely to feel this than non-benefit children (20%). Age was an important factor, and children were more likely to feel that teachers were 'getting at' them as they got older. As we can see from Table 6.9, the effect of age is particularly apparent in the benefit sample, with 39% of teenagers saying that their teachers were 'getting at' them compared with only 14% of pre-teenagers. There was also a significant difference between ages in the non-benefit sample, with 23% of teenagers feeling that their teachers were 'getting at' them compared with 14% of pre-teenagers.

Table 6.9 also shows that whether children and young people were working or not was significant for benefit children and young people, although not for the non-benefit children and young people. Nearly half (44%) of the benefit children and young people who were working felt that their teachers were always 'getting at' them, compared with only one fifth (22%) of benefit children and young people who were not working. There was no significant difference between those not working in either sample. But benefit children and young people who were working were significantly more likely to feel that their teachers were 'getting at' them than were those who were working in non-benefit families.

Table 6.9: Children's belief that teachers are 'getting at' them, by benefit receipt, age and work status (%)

	Benefit		Non-benefit		All	
Teachers 'get at' me						
Agree	28		20		21	
Disagree	72		80		79	
Base (100%)	(114)		(606)		(720)	
Age group	Pre-teen	Teen	Pre-teen	Teen	Pre-teen	Teen
Agree	14	39	14	23	14	25
Disagree	86	61	86	77	86	75
Base (100%)	(49)	(65)	(229)	(377)	(278)	(442)
Children working	Yes	No	Yes	No	Yes	No
Agree	44	22	23	18	26	19
Disagree	56	78	77	82	74	81
Base[a] (100%)	(34)	(76)	(179)	(418)	(213)	(494)

[a] Base numbers of children working are reduced due to 13 non-responses overall.

Source: Author's own analysis of BHPYS (1997, Wave 7)

Do children care about what their teachers think of them?

This section looks at children's feelings about their teacher's perceptions of them. This taps directly into children's notions of themselves as pupils and the value of their relationships with their teachers. Children were asked to say whether they agreed or disagreed with the statement: 'I don't care what teachers think of me'. Table 6.10 shows that the majority (69%) of children in the sample disagreed with the statement, with only 31% agreeing. However, benefit children were much more likely than the other children to agree that they did not care what teachers thought of them. Nearly half of all benefit children (48%) agreed that they did not care, compared to less than a third (28%) of children who were not in benefit households. Receipt of benefit alone appeared to be the main factor underlying these responses. There were no significant effects from age and gender, although there was from whether or not children and young people were working.

As we can see from Table 6.10, over two thirds of the benefit children who were working (67%) say that they did not care what teachers thought of them, compared to just over two fifths (40%) of non-working benefit children. There is no significant difference between working and non-working children who are not in families in receipt of benefit. Furthermore, benefit children who were working (67%) were significantly more likely to say that they did not care what their teachers thought of them, compared with non-benefit children (30%) who were working.

To summarise, this section of the analysis reveals a disturbing discord between benefit children and young people and their teachers. Benefit children were significantly more likely than other children to feel that their teachers were 'getting at' them, particularly teenagers, and those children who were working. Coupled with this, they were also significantly more likely to say that they did not care what their teachers thought of them, than other children.

Table 6.10: Whether children care what teachers think of them, by benefit receipt and work status (%)

	Benefit		**Non-benefit**		**All**	
Don't care what teachers think						
Agree	48		28		31	
Disagree	52		72		69	
Base (100%)	(114)		(606)		(720)	
Children working	Yes	No	Yes	No	Yes	No
Agree	67	40	30	27	35	29
Disagree	33	60	70	73	65	71
Base[a] (100%)	(34)	(76)	(179)	(418)	(213)	(494)

[a] Base numbers of children working are reduced due to 13 non-responses overall.

Source: Author's own analysis of BHPYS (1997, Wave 7)

Children's and young people's perceptions of school

In this section, we explore whether benefit children have different perceptions of themselves at school to their non-benefit counterparts, and look at what role children feel their parents have in their education.

How do children and young people feel about their schoolwork?

First, children were asked how they felt about their schoolwork. Table 6.11 shows that over 80% of children said that they were happy with their schoolwork. However, benefit children were significantly more likely to feel indifferent or unhappy with their schoolwork than other children. Eleven per cent of benefit children were unhappy with their schoolwork compared with 5% of non-benefit children. Gender was also a significant factor affecting how benefit children felt about their schoolwork.

In general girls were happier with their schoolwork than boys, and this is reflected in previous research on pupils' attitudes to school, which found that girls tend to show more positive attitudes towards school and schoolwork than boys (Keys and Fernandes, 1993; Barber, 1996). Benefit boys were the most likely to be indifferent to their work (26%), compared with non-benefit boys (14%) and girls (9%). There was no significant difference between girls and boys among non-benefit children, and no significant differences in perceptions between the benefit girls and the non-benefit girls. However, non-benefit boys were significantly more likely (81%) to feel happy about their schoolwork than benefit boys (64%). Therefore, while gender was a factor, the influence of benefit receipt was particularly apparent for boys.

Table 6.11: How children feel about their schoolwork, by benefit receipt and gender (%)

	Benefit		Non-benefit		All	
Feel about schoolwork						
Happy	70		83		81	
Neither happy nor unhappy	19		12		13	
Unhappy	11		5		6	
Base (100%)	(114)		(606)		(720)	
Gender	Girls	Boys	Girls	Boys	Girls	Boys
Happy	77	64	85	81	84	78
Neither happy nor unhappy	9	26	9	14	9	16
Unhappy	13	10	6	5	7	6
Base (100%)	(53)	(61)	(297)	(309)	(350)	(370)

Source: Author's own analysis of BHPYS (1997, Wave 7)

Table 6.12: The importance of doing well at school, by benefit receipt (%)

	Benefit	Non-benefit	All
How much it means to do well at school			
A lot	89	95	94
Not much	11	5	6
Base (100%)	(114)	(606)	(720)

Source: Author's own analysis of BHPYS (1997, Wave 7)

The importance of doing well at school

This next question explores how important children themselves feel it is to do well at school. Previous studies of pupils' views about doing well at school have shown that a high percentage of pupils believed that it was important to do well at school, to improve credentials and employment prospects (Blatchford, 1996; Campaign for Learning, 1998). Table 6.12 shows that the majority of the children (94%) agreed that it meant a lot to them to do well at school.

However, benefit children were significantly less likely to feel it was important than the others. Eleven per cent of benefit children said that it did not mean much to do well at school, compared with 5% of non-benefit children. Although these are small percentages, they represent a significant core of benefit children and young people who are not as engaged with their education as they could be. Exploration of other factors, such as age and gender, that could be influencing children's responses revealed no significant effects. Thus we have seen that there are small but important percentages of benefit children who are significantly detached in their responses to doing well at school, attending school and to the quality of their relationships with their teachers. To explore these factors further, analysis focused on whether children who were truanting were also those children who felt that it was not important to do well at school, and whether children who said that their teachers were getting at them had a similar response to schoolwork.

Table 6.13 shows that there were significant differences between benefit children who did or did not truant and between children who did or did not feel that their teachers were always getting at them, and their attitudes to doing well at school. These were also reflected to a lesser degree in the rest of the sample. Although there is some overlap between those children who truanted and those who felt that their teachers were getting at them, they are not all the same group of children.

We can see from Table 6.13 that nearly half (45%) of benefit children who were truanting felt that it was not important to do well at school, compared with only 2% of benefit children who were not truanting. In the rest of the sample, a similar picture emerges, although the differences are not as substantial as in the benefit sample (13% compared with 3%).

Table 6.13: The importance of doing well at school, by children truanting and feeling teachers are always 'getting at' them (%)

	Benefit		Non-benefit		All	
Truanting	Yes	No	Yes	No	Yes	No
How much it means to do well at school						
A lot	55	98	87	97	81	97
Not much	45	2	13	3	19	3
Base (100%)	(22)	(92)	(88)	(517)	(110)	(610)
Teachers 'get at' me	Yes	No	Yes	No	Yes	No
How much it means to do well at school						
A lot	69	97	83	98	80	98
Not much	31	3	17	2	20	2
Base (100%)	(32)	(82)	(118)	(488)	(150)	(570)

Source: Author's own analysis of BHPYS (1997, Wave 7)

Of those children who said that their teachers were 'getting at' them, nearly a third (31%) of benefit children stated that it did not mean much to do well at school, compared with only 3% of benefit children who did not feel that their teachers were getting at them. Again, these findings are also reflected in the non-benefit sample, although the differences are not as great. These figures show a worrying link between children's perceptions of themselves at school and their understanding of the importance of academic achievement.

Parental involvement at school

Parental interest in children's school lives are believed to play a key role in children's aspirations and educational achievement. A review of research by Keys and Fernandes (1993) found a clear link between negative attitudes to school and lack of parental support and interest. Parental involvement in school, particularly in disadvantaged areas, is a key principle of the current Labour administration's education policies, including Early Excellence Centres and Education Action Zones[8] (DfEE, 1997).

To explore the extent of parents' involvement with their children's schoolwork, children in the BHPYS sample were asked whether their parents checked on how well they were doing at school. Their responses were coded in two ways: either 'They watch me very closely' or 'They prefer me to be independent'. As Table 6.14 shows, the majority of the children felt that their parents were watching them closely (54%). However, when benefit children are separated from the others a different picture emerges. Only 40% of benefit children felt that their parents were watching their progress at school closely compared with 57% of non-benefit children. Further exploration of the benefit sample reveals that age and gender are not significant explanatory variables. However, in the non-benefit sample age and gender are significant factors.

Table 6.14 shows that pre-teenage children in non-benefit households (65%) are significantly more likely than teenage children (51%) to say that their parents watch them very closely to check on how well they are doing at school. This would seem like an age-based progression related to children becoming more independent in general. Younger children may feel that their parents are watching them closely because pre-teenage years are the time when children first attend secondary school, and there is a lot of attention directed towards both children and parents from the school itself. However, this effect is not as evident or significant among benefit children. Less than half (45%) of the benefit pre-teenagers said that their parents were watching them closely at school, compared with 65% of non-benefit pre-teenagers. Equally, benefit teenagers were significantly more likely to say that their parents preferred them to be independent than non-benefit teenagers and pre-teenagers.

A similar picture emerges when the issue of gender is explored. Table 6.14 shows that there was no significant difference between girls and boys in the benefit sample. However, in households not on benefits, boys were more likely than girls to say that their parents were watching them closely at school. There were no differences between girls, but between the boys only 39% of benefit boys said that their parents were watching them closely, compared with 63% of non-benefit boys. It would appear that in families that do not receive benefits, the boys felt they were more closely watched than the girls and younger children were more closely watched than older children. However, neither of these factors influenced whether or not benefit children said they were being closely

Table 6.14: Parents check on how well children are doing at school, by benefit receipt, age and gender (%)

	Benefit		Non-benefit		All	
Parents check on how well children are doing at school						
Watch me very closely	40		57		54	
Prefer me to be independent	60		43		46	
Base (100%)	(113)		(596)		(709)	
Age group	Pre-teen	Teen	Pre-Teen	Teen	Pre-teen	Teen
Watch me very closely	45	36	65	51	62	49
Prefer me to be independent	55	64	35	49	38	51
Base[a] (100%)	(49)	(64)	(228)	(368)	(277)	(432)
Gender	Girls	Boys	Girls	Boys	Girls	Boys
Watch me very closely	42	39	51	63	49	59
Prefer me to be independent	58	61	49	37	51	41
Base[a] (100%)	(52)	(61)	(291)	(306)	(343)	(367)

[a] Eleven missing cases.

Source: Author's own analysis of BHPYS (1997, Wave 7)

watched at school, and overall they were most likely to say that their parents preferred them to be independent. Nevertheless, these findings should be viewed with some reservations, as there is considerable potential for ambiguity in the question. In addition, children are active agents in their parents' involvement in school life, and while they may initiate and facilitate the parents' involvement and interest in their school life, they may also evade and resist it, or even seek to protect them from it (Alldred et al, 2000).

Children's and young people's perceptions of leaving school

The UK has one of the highest percentages in the OECD countries of young people leaving school at the statutory school-leaving age (*The Guardian*, 2000). Nearly 10% of 16- to 18-year-olds are not in education, employment or training at any one time (DfEE, 1999). This final question focused on whether children felt they would be leaving school at the age of 16, or staying on to go to sixth form or to college. It also recorded children who did not know what they were going to do.

Table 6.15 shows that overall 13% of children expected to leave school at the age of 16, 67% said they would stay on at college or sixth form and 20% did not know what they would be doing. However, as before, the responses from the benefit children were very different to other children. A quarter of the benefit children (25%) responded that they would be leaving school at the age of 16 compared with only 11% of non-benefit children. Two fifths of the benefit children (43%) felt that they would go to sixth form or college compared with nearly three quarters (72%) of non-benefit children. It was also apparent that benefit children expressed a much higher degree of uncertainty about

Table 6.15: Leaving school at the age of 16, or staying on, by benefit receipt and age (%)

	Benefit		Non-benefit		All	
Leaving school/staying on?						
Leaving at age 16	25		11		13	
Staying on at sixth form/college	43		72		67	
Don't know	32		17		20	
Base (100%)	(114)		(606)		(720)	
Age group	Pre-teen	Teen	Pre-teen	Teen	Pre-teen	Teen
Leaving at age 16	17	31	11	10	12	13
Staying on at sixth form/college	37	48	67	75	62	71
Don't know	46	21	22	15	26	16
Base (100%)	(49)	(65)	(229)	(377)	(278)	(442)

Source: Author's own analysis of BHPYS (1997, Wave 7)

their future, with a third of them (32%) not knowing what they would be doing at the age of 16, compared with only 17% of non-benefit children.

As might be expected, there was a significant difference in responses according to age. As Table 6.15 shows, the younger age group of children in both benefit and non-benefit households were more likely to feel unsure about what they would do at the age of 16. As benefit children grow older, they are more likely to say that they would leave school at the age of 16 than when they were younger. This is not reflected in the non-benefit sample, where the percentage remains steady between pre-teenagers and teenagers. Only 17% of pre-teenage benefit children felt that they would leave school at the age of 16, but this rises to 31% of benefit teenagers. Furthermore, pre-teenage benefit children were substantially more likely to say that they did not know what they would do at the age of 16 (46%), than were the pre-teenage non-benefit children (22%). There was also a significant difference between benefit and non-benefit teenagers, with three quarters (75%) of non-benefit teenagers saying that they would stay on at school compared with less than half (48%) of the benefit teenagers.

To summarise, as in the previous sections, benefit children appear to experience the school environment very differently to their non-benefit counterparts. They are more likely to feel indifferent or unhappy about their schoolwork, with boys being the most likely to feel indifferent and the girls more likely to feel unhappy. They are also significantly more likely than non-benefit children to indicate that doing well at school is not that important. It was also apparent that those children who were already reporting problems with their school, through truanting, or feeling that their teachers were 'getting at' them were significantly more likely than other children to disparage doing well at school. Benefit children indicated that their parents did not watch them as closely at school, and they were significantly more likely to say that they would leave school at the age of 16, or were uncertain about what they would do.

Summary

In the first section of the analysis, we looked at how children and young people were actually experiencing their lives at school. Although suspension and expulsion from school is generally the exception rather than the rule, there are clear signs that school suspensions are rising and that this is rapidly becoming an area of major concern and a significant factor in the danger of children experiencing social exclusion (SEU, 1998c). In the findings, children's and young people's responses revealed that living in a family in receipt of benefits was a significant factor in whether they reported being suspended or expelled. There were also clear differences in gender and age, with teenagers and boys being far more likely than pre-teenagers and girls to say they had been suspended or expelled. These findings were also echoed in the section about truancy, which found that benefit receipt was a significant factor in whether children reported truanting from school. Benefit children were more likely than non-benefit children to say they truanted frequently. As might be expected, older children reported the most truancy; however, an interesting finding was that children who were working were nearly twice as likely as children who did not work to report that they truanted. An exploration of worries about bullying revealed that benefit children are more likely than others to worry 'a lot' about bullying. Gender was also a major factor in whether children worried about bullying and girls were the most likely to worry 'a lot'. These findings reveal that, even taking other factors into account, benefit children were experiencing school differently from their peers.

The second section examined children's relationships with their teachers. Although most children appeared to like their teachers, analysis of their perceptions of whether teachers liked them revealed a different picture. Benefit children were significantly more likely to say that their teachers were 'getting at' them than were other children. Older children were also more likely to feel this, as were benefit children who were working. When children responded to the question about whether they cared what teachers thought about them, a clear divide was apparent with benefit children, especially those who were working, the most likely to say that they did not care what their teachers thought of them.

The final section explored children's perceptions of school itself. When children were asked how they felt about their schoolwork a significant difference was apparent between benefit children and non-benefit children. Benefit children, particularly boys, were the most likely to express indifference towards their work. They were also significantly more likely to say that doing well at school was unimportant. How important children feel success is at school may well reflect their perceptions of themselves as learners and may affect the outcome of the learning process. Children who say it is not very important to do well at school may well be disengaged at some level from the potential benefits for them of education. Analysis revealed that those children who said that their teachers were getting at them, and those who were truanting, were significantly more likely to say that doing well at school was not important; this was especially so for benefit children.

Parents are being expected to play an increasingly active role in their children's education, and one of the ways in which they can be involved is by keeping a close eye on their children's progress and academic well-being. When children were asked whether their parents watched them closely at school or preferred them to be independent, the findings showed that benefit children were significantly more likely to say that their parents preferred them to be independent than to watch them closely. The final part of the analysis concerned whether children felt they would stay on at school or leave at the age of 16, and indicated that benefit children were more likely than others to leave at the age of 16. They also had a higher degree of uncertainty about what they would do. Age was a significant factor and as benefit children got older, they were more likely to say they would leave at the age of 16 than when they were younger. This may well reflect the growing loss of confidence and lack of expectations that are evident from the rest of the findings.

Family Credit children and young people

The responses of children and young people from families in receipt of Family Credit were also included in the analysis, where preliminary analysis had indicated they had a significantly different profile to both benefit and non-benefit children. However, the sample size was too small to draw any robust conclusions from the data[9]. Nevertheless, it is of interest to explore the responses of these children and young people, particularly in the light of increasing numbers of children and young people living in families in receipt of in-work benefits[10]. The findings show that they were, perhaps surprisingly, the group most likely to report being suspended or expelled from school. The LOGIT model shows that being in a Family Credit household raises the odds significantly for being suspended or expelled. They were also significantly more likely to say that they were truanting from school than other children. These findings indicate that Family Credit children's experiences of school should give some cause for concern.

Lessons to be drawn from the quantitative study

The value of a large children's data set is clear from this study, particularly as the analysis has revealed the important differences between benefit children and their peers. The data relating to benefit children are unequivocal and these findings raise critical questions about the assumed parity of experience between children at school. They indicate that children living in households receiving low-income means-tested benefits are having qualitatively different experiences at school to their non-benefit peers. For a minority, but a substantial number of benefit children, they expose a situation of disquiet and unhappiness with school, reflected in children's more problematic relationships with their teachers, their fears of bullying and their perceptions of school as an academic environment from which they are substantially disengaged.

Notes

[1] The latest data available at the time the qualitative fieldwork was carried out.

[2] Means-tested benefits referred to in this instance are Income-related Jobseeker's Allowance and Income Support.

[3] See the Appendix for an overview of the BHPYS, information about data collection and utilisation.

[4] For analysis purposes, children were coded into two age groups: pre-teenage (11-12 years) and teenage (13-15 years).

[5] Jobseeker's Allowance was included to ensure a large enough sample size for analysis.

[6] Children and young people living in IS/JSA households will be identified as benefit children.

[7] A LOGIT model is a logistic regression model. It is used where the dependent variable is dichotomous – in this case expelled or suspended yes or no – and the independent variables can be entered simultaneously. It is particularly valuable for an analysis like this where one factor – Family Credit – is sufficiently small so as to affect the significance of chi-square tests. The model creates a *logit* or *log* of the odds which is the (natural log of the) probability of being in one group divided by the probability of being in the other group.

[8] Early Education Centres offer a one-stop integrated education and day care service for young children and their parents. Education Action Zones are local partnerships in disadvantaged areas which are intended to improve the quality of teaching and learning, to promote social inclusion and to provide better family and pupil support.

[9] Family Credit sample was 45 cases – unweighted.

[10] Family Credit has now been replaced by Working Families' Tax Credit, which is one of the cornerstones of the Labour government's anti-poverty initiatives.

SEVEN

Childhood poverty and social exclusion: incorporating children's perspectives

Throughout this study, the children have been open and informative about their lives, and we have gained an invaluable insight into their everyday experiences, and the issues that concern them. In this final chapter we reflect on those insights and explore how incorporating the perspectives of children and young people from low-income and disadvantaged families into policy and practice can contribute to a greater understanding of childhood poverty and social exclusion.

What we have learnt from listening to children and young people

Listening to the accounts of children and young people has revealed how the effects of poverty and disadvantage can permeate every aspect of their lives; from the material and more quantifiable aspects of their needs, to the social and emotional requirements so important for children, both in childhood and beyond. The first area of concern highlighted by the qualitative findings (Chapter Three) was children's and young people's limited access to their own autonomously controlled economic resources, particularly in the form of pocket money. Just over a quarter of the study sample received pocket money on a regular basis, and some of these children received it only conditionally, in return for household chores. Nearly three quarters of the children and young people in the study did not receive any pocket money at all, or received it only on an irregular basis. As we would expect, many of those children and young people who did receive pocket money spent it on sweets and treats. However, they were also managing their money in a socially productive way, saving up to purchase clothes, items for school, bus fares and so on. In this way they were able to go some way towards sustaining themselves in areas where they were experiencing considerable disadvantage. For these children and young people, pocket money served as a vital socioeconomic resource, facilitating their capacity for sustaining social interaction and engagement with friends, and providing them – albeit in small measure – with an element of economic autonomy and control in an environment that is characterised by scarcity and constraint. For those without pocket money, work appeared to be the main way to resolve their complete lack of independent income (see below). However, of greatest concern were those children and young people (two fifths of the study sample) who had neither pocket money, nor income from work, leaving them without any economic autonomy, and greatly restricted opportunities to develop economic competence and financial control.

There was a clear link between the absence of pocket money and involvement in work. Overall, nearly half of the study sample were either working or had been in work. Those who were not working, especially those above the legal working age, showed a keen desire to get work as soon as possible. Access to work for many young people was clearly constrained by a lack of opportunities and transport, and there were also evident tensions between working and children's school and social lives, especially for young people who were doing more than one job or working long hours. We have little understanding of what the meanings and significance of work are for children, least of all for children from low-income families. What is known has been largely framed in a discourse of work as a 'life-style' issue (Mizen et al, 1999), with children's main motivation towards work being the desire to have money to buy more consumer goods (White, 1996). However, these children highlighted work as being much more than an issue of money; it was also an issue of autonomy, independence and choice. As well as the obvious motivation to share in the consumer culture of their peers, children's and young people's work also played an important role in their families' economies. Several children in lone-parent families were helping their mothers with money, and even where children were not directly contributing to the household budget, they were freeing household money for other needs. In addition, it also enabled some children to pay for their own school trips and other essential items at school.

The importance of access to affordable transport was also revealed as a critical issue for children and young people from low-income families. In general, children's access to transport is already mediated by adults, and this can constrain their freedom and autonomy. However, life in a low-income household added a further dimension to issues of mobility and access. Nearly half of the children and young people in the study were without access to private transport. As a consequence, adequate and affordable public transport was essential if they were to be able to sustain wider networks of friends and to participate in shared social activities. Lack of transport also affected reciprocity, and the everyday exchange of lifts and favours that make up much of children's social lives; enabling children to share lifts to clubs, have children over to tea and take them home again and so on. Children in large families and lone-parent families, particularly those in rural areas, were especially vulnerable to restricted mobility and heavily reliant on expensive and inadequate public transport. In the light of these findings, the role of public transport as an affordable and viable resource for children and young people on a low income assumes considerable importance.

The importance of friendships for children from low-income families, and the value of developing and sustaining satisfactory social relationships, were explored in Chapter Four. Throughout the study it is evident that children have a particular need for friendships and peer networks, that for them, friendship is a valued and precious resource. Friends were seen variously as protective, reliable, an alternative source of support from family, and as confidants and problem solvers. However, difficulties in making and sustaining social relationships were apparent, and could have severe repercussions for the children's capacity to maintain adequate social inclusion, and to develop their human and social capital.

Friendships were seen as protective, particularly by boys, because without friends they felt especially vulnerable to bullying and exclusion. Fears of loneliness and social isolation were very real, and some children were clearly very isolated. This is an area in which children struggled particularly hard to maintain an acceptable level of social involvement. Lack of financial resources to participate in shared social events with friends, restricted access to transport, the cost of transport, lack of space and an inability to be reciprocal, are all factors identified as damaging to children and young people from low-income families' social viability. For many children, friendships made at school are valued but harder to sustain beyond the confines of school itself. Yet, in many ways, school represents these children's greatest opportunity to meet a cross-section of children and to develop wider social networks.

For many children the value of school as an opportunity to meet with friends was overshadowed by their experiences of bullying. Over half of the children in the qualitative study said that they had been bullied, and said that they had little faith in the school's capacity to stop it. Experiencing bullying can be particularly painful and damaging to children's well-being and self-esteem. Fear of being bullied, of being different, or in any way standing out, was apparent throughout the interviews, and is reflected in the children's endeavours to find the resources to dress in the 'right' clothes, and to join in social and leisure activities with their peers.

Clothes were singled out by children and young people as especially important for their self-identity and for social protection. Having adequate clothing helped children and young people to fit in and to be accepted as part of their social groups. Having the 'right' clothes allayed fears of bullying and were also seen as valuable for developing self-esteem and confidence. Older children were more concerned than the younger ones about 'inappropriate dressing', and this indicates that these issues may become particularly important for children during their early teenage years, and their entry into secondary education. The school environment itself, where school uniform could be considered to have a protective effect, is revealed as fraught with social demands, and with subtle nuances of clothing expectations. The loss of school uniform grants has meant that pressures to maintain an adequate standard of school clothing has been increased, and there was an acute awareness of the tensions between the parents' difficulties in providing the children with a school uniform, and the children's need to blend in with the other children. Special days, such as 'mufti days', were revealed as placing extra pressures on these children, an outcome far from their original intention.

There was also considerable cause for concern about the degree of participation and inclusion children were able to sustain at school. In the qualitative section of the study, children in families in receipt of Income Support highlighted the importance of school for them as a social space to meet with friends, and this was especially so for children living in rural areas.

Given the social significance of school to children and young people from low-income families, it was disturbing to find that there were considerable constraints on the children's ability to engage fully in their school's social and academic life. In particular, the social value derived from shared experiences on school trips and outings was being denied to many of them, with over half of the children and young people in the study unable to go on school trips with any regularity. Many of these children were fearful of being left behind, and consequently excluded. Many of them were not going away for holidays with their families either, and therefore the chance of going away with the school on a trip assumed a particular importance. Children and young people also revealed their concerns about the costs of participating generally at school. School bags, stationery, books, and so on are all problematic to afford, and GCSE projects in particular were singled out as an area where young people felt that their resources fell well below those of their peers. This had led to fears that they would be unable to produce the quality of work required, which would adversely affect their examination marks.

The final chapter of qualitative findings drew on children's accounts of their home lives and their perception of the impact poverty has made on their lives. An exploration of the opportunities presented for social and leisure activities revealed an extremely impoverished social environment, characterised by inadequate provision of shared peer activities. The cost of participation and lack of access to transport acted as further constraints on the children's capacity to make use of what little was available to them. Concerns about the quality of their neighbourhood environments revealed fears about enhanced visibility and stigma for some children and young people from rural areas and worries about safety and traffic for children living in urban areas.

Children's perceptions of need satisfaction within their families were also explored. Initially there appeared to be clear differences between those who would ask their parent/s for something expensive and those who would not. However, exploring the issue further revealed that even those that asked for something had very little expectation that they would receive it; in essence few children actually felt that they could ask for something and get it. The evidence here is that children's perceptions of need satisfaction within their families are highly complex. The findings expose the difference for these children between asking and getting, and between their perceptions of what is possible, and what is not. Underpinning their understandings are a complexity of interactions and negotiations with parents, involving realistic assessments of their family's financial situations and the potential for realisation of needs through alternative strategies devised through work.

Holidays away together are an important and accepted part of family life.

Yet the children in this study were experiencing very restricted opportunities to go away with their families. Half of the study had not been on a holiday of any kind in recent years and some had never been away on holiday. External sources of support for holidays were sometimes forthcoming; some children from lone-parent families were getting holidays with their non-resident parent, and two-parent families were sometimes able to access charitable support for holidays. However, none of these options was sufficiently reliable or satisfactory to ensure these children a holiday with any regularity. This meant that children were also very aware of their friends going away on holiday during the school summer break, while they were left behind.

When exploring children's and young people's perceptions of the impact poverty had made on their lives in general, nearly three quarters of the study sample felt very strongly that their lives had been changed by living on a low income. Several children traced their problems back to the upheavals of family breakdown or illness and disability, which had precipitated their experience of poverty, and reflected on how their lives had changed. Many children felt that their friendships had been compromised and affected and that they were in danger of being excluded through an inability to meet with friends and to share in the accepted social events. Some children were particularly fearful of the social repercussions of being seen as poor and somehow different. Alongside their reflections about poverty, children also talked about their worries, and these indicated that many children were very concerned about their parent's situation, particularly their health, and their capacity to pay their bills and to manage their money. Several children were also worried about not having enough money for their own needs. A few of the children appeared to be particularly insecure and expressed worries about their future lives, and what would happen to them as they got older if they were not able to manage or to fit in.

Finally, children talked about what they would change in their lives if they could. It was interesting to note that not all the children were able to imagine their lives any differently. But where they did, children did not have a long wish list of unattainable goods, but rather, many of their responses reflected the realities of their lives and their environment. For example, some were living in overcrowded homes and wished merely for more space, and some wished for an improvement in the health of a disabled parent or sibling. The biggest areas for change were opportunities for children to see more of their friends and to be able to participate in shared social activities. Over a quarter of the children talked about the difference having more money would make to their lives, and to their security.

Chapter Six presented the findings from a quantitative analysis of a large-scale data set. This presented an opportunity to compare the lives of a large sample of children and young people from low-income families (those receiving Income Support or Jobseeker's Allowance) with those who were not receiving benefits. This focused particularly on perceptions and experiences of school, and was a larger and more representative sample than the qualitative study.

Nevertheless, the findings supported and confirmed the findings of the in-depth interviews.

Many children and young people from benefit families – those living in families in receipt of Income Support/Jobseeker's Allowance – were evidently having a qualitatively different experience of school to other children. These children were significantly more likely to say that they had been expelled or suspended from school, and that they had truanted. They were also significantly more concerned about bullying. Their relationships with their teachers appeared to be more problematic than those of non-benefit children, and perceptions of the value of school to their futures revealed disturbing signs of disengagement. They were more likely to feel indifferent or unhappy with their schoolwork than non-benefit children, and less likely than them to say that it was important to do well at school. Young people in benefit families indicated that they did not feel that their parents watched them very closely at school, but preferred them instead to be independent. In the climate of increased social and policy pressure for parents to be more closely involved in their children's school lives, this would appear to indicate that there is a lack of parental involvement on the part of these parents.

The final part of the analysis concerned whether young people felt that they would stay on at school or leave at the age of 16. Here the benefit children were more likely than non-benefit children to say they would be leaving at the age of 16, and this was particularly so for the older children. The quantitative data reveals significant differences between benefit children and their non-benefit counterparts, across a broad range of school issues. The picture that emerges is of children's disillusionment and disengagement, both with themselves as students and with the school as a rewarding or inclusive environment.

The importance of mediating factors in understanding children's experiences

There is no 'universal' childhood but many 'childhoods', and children's and young people's lives and experiences will be mediated through a diverse range of other factors (James and Prout, 1997). Throughout the study, certain demographic factors were used to explore potential differences between children. Here we look at those factors and examine what contribution they make to our understanding of these children's lives.

Family type

Overall, there appears to be little substantial difference in the qualitative study between children and young people in lone-parent families and those within two-parent families. Similarities in the duration of poverty between lone-parent families and two-parent families (where there is a disabled family member) appear to be producing similar poverty profiles between children. Some differences have emerged between the different resources lone parents and two-parent families are able to call on, particularly around access to transport and holidays. For children in lone-parent families there is the potential for the non-resident parent to provide resources beyond those available to the parent with care. However, the study reveals that lone-parent children had little expectation of their non-resident parent providing help or support. Where support was forthcoming, it was mainly in kind, through holiday opportunities, rather than in the form of additional money for pocket money and so on. However, the opportunity to have a holiday for a child who would otherwise be unable to have one is significant. This would indicate that non-resident parents have important roles to play in children's social lives and well-being, as well as in their material well-being.

The potential role of non-resident parents as an additional external resource for lone-parent children was echoed in the two-parent families by involvement with charities, due to the presence of disability in the family. Several families had been helped by charities, particularly with holidays. However, as one parent indicated, charitable help is not a reliable source of help, it is often bureaucratic, and the discretionary nature of awards can leave people with unfulfilled needs, and feeling demeaned. For both lone parents and two-parent families, these extra sources of support had often proved problematic and unreliable.

It is interesting to note that children in two-parent families rarely mentioned wider family involvement. However, in lone-parent families grandparents in particular appeared to play a significant role, providing help both in the provision of pocket money and with transport. In the quantitative study, family type was not a significant factor. Within the benefit sample, there were no significant differences evident in the analysis between children in lone-parent and two-parent families, and their experiences of suspensions, truancy, bullying and so on. These are interesting findings, and could suggest that having one or two parents is far less significant in poor children's lives than the experience of poverty itself, particularly over long durations.

Gender

As we would expect, there were some differences between boys and girls in both the qualitative and quantitative studies. In the qualitative study, overall there was little evidential difference between boys and girls. However, in a few areas, notably with regard to clothes and friendship, there were differences. Girls were more articulate about their friendships and appeared to value them more for their supportive and confiding role, rather than for the fun element identified by boys. However, the boys also highlighted the protective role of friends. This may well reflect society's expectations of different genders, and boys may find it much harder to articulate publicly the value they may place on the care and support of their friends. Alternatively, friendship may indeed have different meanings for boys than girls; unfortunately, these are issues we are unable to resolve with this study. Regarding clothes, girls appeared to be marginally more interested in clothes than the boys. However, this was not as great a difference as might be expected and clothes were clearly important for both genders. Girls also appeared to be very concerned and protective of their parents, and in general were more likely than boys to express such concern.

In the quantitative study, there were several apparent differences between gender. In particular, boys were three times as likely as girls to say they had been suspended or expelled from school. Girls were more likely to worry 'a lot' about bullying than boys, although the qualitative study had found no difference between gender in their actual experiences of bullying. Boys also appeared to care less than girls about their schoolwork. However, overall in this part of the study there were remarkably few differences between the responses of boys and girls in the benefit sample. Rather, the differences were between those who were in receipt of benefits and those who were not.

Age

Age is also an important factor to be considered in any understanding of children's and young people's lives. The experiences of a young child may differ considerably from those of an older one. However, this study tried to let children express their own perspectives without making prior judgements or assumptions according to age or developmental theory. In the qualitative study, the children and young people were aged between 10 and 17. There were evidently some differences in perceptions between the younger children and the older ones. However, the overall impressions given were remarkably similar. The impact of age manifested itself most obviously in the degree to which young people felt oppressed by their poverty and their surroundings. As children grew older they appeared to find the restrictions of poverty harder to bear, and they expressed a desire for much greater social involvement and access to the material resources to ensure it.

The experience of childhood is one of transitions and a critical transition would appear to be from junior school to secondary school, with differences most apparent between the ages of 10 to 11 and older children from 12 to 17. Age was also an important factor in children's responses to clothes, and 12 appeared to be a critical age for greater self-awareness and self-esteem. The age group of 10-13 years is one that encompasses considerable social and developmental changes, yet it is a time that is easily overlooked in policy and practice (Madge et al, 2000). Older children were also more likely to work; however, a third of children under the age of 13 were also in work or had been so. Overall, the similarities between children in poverty appeared greater than any dissimilarity according to age.

In the quantitative study, the sample was divided between pre-teenage (11-12) and teenage (13-15) groups, and there were some differences between these two. Teenagers were more likely to say they had been suspended or expelled from school or played truant. Benefit teenagers were also more likely than pre-teenagers to say that they would leave school at the age of 16; this may well reflect a growing disillusionment with school over time, especially in the light of the evidently problematic relationship between benefit children and school. In the other areas of analysis, however, there were no significant differences between these two age groups, with Income Support/Jobseeker's Allowance receipt alone being the strongest explanatory factor. Age is clearly an important factor in children's lives, however, as we have seen from this study; children's experiences of disability, family breakdown and poverty may well influence their lives and shape their experience and needs, well beyond any understanding that a purely developmental perspective on their lives could encompass.

Location

In the qualitative study, the children were drawn from both rural and urban locations[1] to gain an insight into children's lives in two potentially different sociospatial locations. In the analysis, some key differences emerged which are of particular interest. First, children and young people in rural areas indicated that they felt particularly vulnerable and visible at times, particularly with regard to bullying and receiving their free school meals. Rural poverty is often experienced in the midst of plenty, and as such the dangers of social differentiation and stigma is very real. Second, the problems of access to adequate and affordable transport highlighted by children were especially acute for children living in rural areas, where public transport is notoriously expensive and inadequate. This was especially so for such children in lone-parent families, who were the group least likely to have access to private transport. Elsewhere in the study the differences were much less apparent, and children's and young people's opportunities to meet with their friends and so on were equally as constrained in large estates in the inner city as they were in rural villages.

Clearly, the lives of children and young people from low-income families are very diverse and their experiences will be mediated by many factors such as age, gender and ethnicity. There is no homogeneous group of 'poor' children, and although this study sheds considerable light on some of these differences, further research is evidently needed to explore the impact of different life-styles and demographic factors on children's lives. The children in this study were all permanently settled and white, whereas children from different ethnic minority households, Traveller children, and those in Bed & Breakfast accommodation for example, will have their own experiences and concerns to relate. It was also evident that some children in the study appeared to be more protected from the experience of poverty than others and this has important implications for future policies. This is a complex issue and further research is needed to explore the dynamics of these protective factors. In many ways, this research has opened a door into children's lives, but there is still much more to learn. However, there are certain key overarching issues that have been highlighted by the study and these are discussed in the following section.

Key issues arising from the study

The desire to protect: children and young people from low-income families protecting their parents

For most of us the home environment represents a secure base and one in which we anticipate a large degree of fulfilment for our material and social needs. For children the home represents the wellspring of material, social and emotional support. As we have seen, the experiences of children in poverty within their families is an area about which we know very little. The findings from this study have provided a valuable insight into some of these more hidden issues.

Previous research has shown that in low-income families parents are likely to strive to protect their children as far as they can from the worst effects of poverty (Kempson et al, 1994; Middleton et al, 1997; Goode et al, 1998). In particular mothers, especially lone mothers, may go without items or activities to provide things for their children (Middleton et al, 1997). However, what is strikingly apparent from this study is the way in which this need to protect is reciprocal. Children and young people from low-income families are also clearly struggling to protect their parents from the realities of the social and emotional costs of childhood poverty on their lives. This can take many forms: self-denial of needs and wants, moderation of demands, and self-exclusion from social activities such as school trips and clubs. In some cases, parents were clearly aware of their children's strategies, reluctantly accepting that their children were curbing their needs and demands in the face of severely constrained alternatives. In other cases, children and young people were regulating their needs and expectations more covertly. These findings raise concerns about whether children are 'learning to be poor', by restricting their behaviour and aspirations (Shropshire and Middleton, 1999). However, children are sentient actors who are competent and capable of empathising with their parents' needs and perspectives (Brannen et al, 2000). What is evident here is that these children are thoughtful agents who are mindful of their parents' situation, they are aware of the economic realities of their families' lives, and they structure their demands accordingly.

Of particular concern must be the strongly gendered nature of children's protection of their parents; girls were most likely to express concern and the desire to protect their parents, although some boys in lone-mother families were also highly protective. In the case of girls there must be a concern that they are learning gendered patterns of self-denial that are reflected in studies of women from low-income families, where women assume the burden of going without to protect other members of the family (Middleton et al, 1994, 1997; Goode et al, 1998).

Children and young people from low-income families as active social agents

Children and young people are increasingly recognised as active social agents, constructing and making sense of their own lives and experiences (James and Prout, 1997). However, while children and young people from low-income families, living in poverty, are reflexive social agents, their childhoods are also organised by the constraints of poverty. Any understanding of childhood poverty must encompass the discourse, agency and identity of the child, while also recognising the social and material boundaries, constructions and institutions, which shape the experience of being a child from a low-income family.

It is evident from their lucid accounts that the children and young people in this study are not passive victims of their poverty or their environment. They engage with their lives and their circumstances, developing ways and means of participating where and when they can, and utilising alternative strategies of survival and social involvement through work and play. However, they are also engaged in intense social and personal endeavour to maintain social acceptance and social inclusion within the accepted cultural demands of childhood, a struggle that is defined and circumscribed by the material and social realities of their lives. This study indicates that if we are to truly understand the complex dynamics of poverty on children's lives, and their capacity for self-realisation, we need to develop a much greater understanding of children's agency and the meanings and understandings they give to their lives in the context of a restricted social, material and structural environment.

School: exclusion from within

The school environment is increasingly characterised by an intensification of measured academic outcomes through a tightly structured and prescriptive curriculum, which includes heightened control over a pupil's time and activities (Alderson, 1999; James and James, 2001). The social and cultural aspects of school life are in danger of diminishing in importance, and children have generally experienced a reduction in their opportunities for free social interaction during breaks, including the loss of the afternoon break, even though research shows that children value school breaks highly as an opportunity to be with friends (Alderson, 1999; Christensen and James, 2000). The social aspects of school life have been sidelined. For children from low-income families, especially those from rural areas, it needs to be acknowledged that social space at school has a particular salience.

Instrumental in children's capacity to stay socially engaged in times of financial crisis will be the social or institutional environment in which they experience it. Mingione (1997) argues that to understand social exclusion we need to identify not only indicators of poverty but also the institutional processes that bring about exclusion. In this respect, we need to look to the school environment, and the institutional processes within schools, that act to exclude children from their peers. These will of course include economic barriers such as fees for school trips and the costs of school books and so on. However, these disadvantages are exacerbated by institutional processes; an insistence on uniforms and equipment, demanding examination criteria, deposit deadlines, meetings after school with no transport home and overly stigmatising bureaucratic processes of qualification and delivery in welfare support.

An examination of these factors reveals a structural and institutional exclusion, which compounds the social and material disadvantages that children from low-income families are experiencing. From the two sets of data presented in the study, we have a clear picture of considerable disparities between the school lives of children from low-income families and their peers. These factors are intensified by children's awareness of their disadvantage and their inability to access the economic and material resources that are needed for adequate social participation and academic equity. This raises serious questions about the assumed parity of experience between children at school. Exclusion *from* school has long been recognised as a factor in children's likelihood of experiencing social exclusion; what is apparent from this study is that exclusion *within* school may pose an equally grave danger for children from low-income families.

The publication of the Education Green Paper, *Schools, building on success* (DfEE, 2001b), contains an important acknowledgement that poor children are missing out on school opportunities and learning experiences enjoyed by their more affluent peers. Pupil Learning Credits[2] are a welcome initiative which will go some way towards opening up the debate about equity and opportunity within the education system. However, these measures will only address a small part of the disadvantage that children from low-income families and their parents can experience within the education system.

Funding which is only targeted towards schools where there is a high percentage of free school meals does nothing for children from low-income families within most schools, especially for such children and young people in rural schools, where the issue of stigma and difference can be particularly acute. Studies have shown that while schools cannot eliminate social inequalities on their own, they can make a valuable contribution towards enabling children and young people from disadvantaged backgrounds to enjoy a normal school career (Cox, 2000; Nicaise, 2000). Funding needs to be targeted towards all children from low-income families, whatever the circumstances of their schools, ensuring that at the material and financial level, schooling is effectively free, so that wherever possible children and young people are able to fit in and to join in with their peers. Until then the dangers of exclusion *within* school will persist.

Friendships and social networks as a social asset

Friendship plays an important role as a social asset; it is a valuable source of social capital, and an integral part of an increasingly complex and demanding social world. Children's experiences of friendship and their opportunities to make and sustain friendships is critical both for their well-being and self and social identity within childhood (Rubin, 1980), and for their future economic and social needs in adulthood. Friendship for children, as for adults, is an entry point into wider social networks. These are vital to protect against poverty and social exclusion. 6 (1997) has argued that people need to develop complex and diverse social networks which are rich in 'strong' and 'weak' social ties, which provide links to financial and employment opportunities[3]. Social networks also provide social protection at times of transition, and 'network transition poverty' can occur when there is an inability to make the transition to a network configuration suitable for changing needs (6, 1997). For children the movement from childhood dependency to adulthood is experienced as a series of transitions, such as the movement from school to work, from family of origin towards family of destination and so on (see Coles, 1995). Adequate social networks may be crucial for successful negotiation of these transitions.

Children from low-income families are already at risk of network poverty because their families are likely to be detached from social institutions, and experiencing restricted social engagement. They may already be in 'social retreat' (Walker and Park, 1998). Therefore, the value of sustaining children in their social relationships and facilitating their links with wider and more diverse social environments becomes crucial. However, it is clear from the findings of this study that these children are having great difficulty maintaining adequate social participation. Those that do manage to stay linked into social networks through participation at school and involvement in clubs and social activities outside of school, may be better protected against the long-term effects of poverty than others.

Child-centred social exclusion

The notion of social exclusion has potentially much greater power to reveal the multidimensional nature of poverty and disadvantage in childhood than the narrower definition of poverty, which focuses mainly on distributional issues and income inequalities. Social exclusion opens up our understanding of the dynamics of poverty to embrace social relationships, citizenship and the ability to realise citizen's rights and entitlements. As Room (1995, p 6) argues, "social exclusion focuses primarily on relational issues, in other words, inadequate social participation, lack of social integration and lack of power". It is both comprehensive and dynamic (Berghman, 1995), and seeks to capture the processes by which people become detached and isolated from mainstream society, and their capacity for effective economic, social, political and cultural participation is affected (Duffy, 1995).

Children in this study are clearly engaged in a complex social world, the realm of childhood. This has its own social and cultural values and its own social and economic demands, and the pressures on children to fit in and to join in with their peers are considerable. While the notion of social exclusion has the potential to capture and encompass more than just economic security, and labour market issues, it is this *social* aspect of social exclusion that has been the least developed and understood. Moreover, it is clear from these findings that these less tangible, but crucial, aspects of poverty and social exclusion may have much to tell us about the experience of poverty and social exclusion in childhood.

Constraints in participation, and challenges to social well-being, self-esteem, social identity, and social integration, coupled with a reduced capacity to make and sustain adequate social relationships and social networks, are all facets of social exclusion, and are all manifest in these children's accounts of their lives. There is a clear social and material difference between children in poverty and other children. This is evident in these children's limited access to economic and material resources such as pocket money, leisure facilities and transport. But is also apparent in their restricted social environments, and the constraints on their opportunities for social engagement, and sustaining wider social networks. Children and young people are driven by the same consumer culture as adults, and the social imperative is increasingly to present a visible display of ownership of consumer goods, including designer labels and fashion accessories (Middleton et al, 1994). Children and young people from low-income families in this study expressed great concern about looking different, being unable to fit in, or to join in with others, and their awareness of the social implications of these differences. In particular the labels that society attach to poor children will have a profound impact on how children see themselves and on how other children see them. Increased residualisation and means-testing of benefits has led to a heightened risk of social stigma, and this can be compounded by the stigma attached to lone parenthood or unemployment, and so on. These factors are reflected in the sharp awareness of children that they might been seen as different and find themselves isolated and marginalised.

Developing a child-centred understanding of social exclusion, firmly located in childhood, has the advantage of being a child measure rather than an adult or household measure of poverty and exclusion. Children experience the realities of poverty and social exclusion in the immediacy of childhood, not in relation to their future status as adults. However, much of the government's recent policies have been focused on children as future investments, or concerns about children and young people as threats to social order and stability (see SEU 1998a, 1998b, 1998c, 1999). Children and young people have tended to be seen mainly as a future resource, as a form of human capital, to be protected and developed as the adults of the future. As a consequence, the policies adopted by government have taken a particular form. Initiatives such as the ConneXions Strategy for 13- to 19-year-olds, intended to provide 'the best start in life for every young person' has a heavy bias towards a future employment agenda (DfEE, 2000). Its stated concern is to "ensure that more and more young people ... make a successful transition from adolescence to adulthood and working life" (DfEE, 2000, Foreword). The government's child poverty strategy also stresses the value of children as the adults of the future, aiming to ensure that children are given "the tools they will need to succeed in the adult world" (DSS, 1999a, p 1). As Prout (2000) argues, the government has drawn heavily on poverty studies that link childhood poverty with poor adult outcomes to inform its child poverty strategies. The central focus of its policies are "on the better adult lives that will, it is predicted, emerge from reducing child poverty. It is not on the better lives that children will lead as children" (Prout, 2000, p 305). Clearly, a concern about the future of children and young people as they make the transition from childhood to adulthood is not misplaced. But equally, a concern for the quality of life and the experiences of children in childhood is essential if childhood poverty and social exclusion is to be addressed.

Building on what we know: policy recommendations

There can be a tension between those needs identified by children and those that may be identified by adults. Adults may well not value the things that these children identify as important social needs. Previous research has shown that issues that preoccupy adults about children and young people, such as drug taking and violence on the streets, are not the issues identified by children and young people themselves as the most salient in their lives; the children are more likely to be concerned about loss, bullying and conflicts with peers, family and teachers (Hill, 1999). In this study, we are presented with issues relating to the everyday lives of children and young people from low-income families, and they have clearly identified areas for concern, such as friendship, clothing expectations, school inclusion and shared peer group participation. These represent critical areas in children's social lives and in their social development. Thus, the findings present a challenge: how should we respond to children's concerns, and how can we ensure that welfare targeted at children and young people from low-income families reaches them and addresses their needs? The following section is built on the understanding and insight gained from these findings, and sets out the policy recommendations necessary to address some of the features of exclusion and disadvantage that children have highlighted.

Fundamental to any measures that seek to address the impact of poverty as outlined by these children must be the push towards more adequate levels of benefit provision. As we have seen, the recent up-rating of Income Support premiums for children in recent budgets have increased the Income Support level considerably (see Chapter Three). However, although this brings income levels closer to basic needs, they are still well below the average. There has been no up-rating of adult needs in Income Support levels, and therefore these extra income measures for children will of necessity be diluted, as children's needs cannot be separated out from their families. Many families in poverty are also in severe debt and repayments taken by the Social Fund and utilities, for instance, will serve to depress further the incomes of those families (Millar and Ridge, 2001). Lone-parent families are the most likely to receive Social Fund, and fuel and water deductions from their Income Support payments[4] (DSS, 2000b).

Furthermore, welcome though the recent increases are, they are still undermined by a fundamental inequity within the benefits system, as families on Income Support are penalised by having their Child Benefit deducted from their Income Support payments. As Child Benefit is a universal benefit given as a right to all parents as an acknowledgement of the extra costs of bringing up children, it represents in some ways a child's badge of citizenship (Lister, 1990). Future plans to introduce a new integrated support for children, the Child Tax Credit in 2003, would provide an ideal opportunity to remove this iniquitous state of affairs and extend the support of the Child Tax Credit to all low-income families, by disregarding Child Benefit, regardless of whether they are receiving an in-work benefit or Income Support/Jobseeker's Allowance. This would go some way towards acknowledging the needs and rights of all children from low-income families, as well as addressing some of the income disparities between Income Support/Jobseeker's Allowance families and others.

However, not all poor children are living in families in receipt of the means-tested benefits that the government has uprated. Analysis by the Institute for Fiscal Studies (Brewer et al, 2002) point to a significant proportion of poor children (around two in five) that live in families that do not receive the uprated benefits and are therefore not benefiting from the current provisions. They go on to suggest that even in order to reduce child poverty by half in the future, the government would have to commit itself to a permanent increase in spending for children of 1% of GDP (Brewer et al, 2002). This would represent a significant investment in the lives of children and would entail a much greater social and political commitment to an equitable distribution of society's resources towards children. To ensure the rights of children to enjoy a childhood free of poverty, difficult political choices about taxation and the redistribution of wealth would have to be made, and children's rights would have to prevail over the competing demands of other more powerful social groups. At present, there is no indication that the government is prepared to commit itself to such a course of action.

In addition to increased financial redistribution towards children, many of the issues highlighted by children could be usefully addressed through greater provision of welfare in kind. Because we cannot separate children from their families, they are always vulnerable to principles of 'less eligibility' which are directed at maintaining the work incentive for their parents. However, child-centred, non-stigmatising welfare provision which is targeted directly at children, and informed by their own perceptions of need, may have a valuable role in facilitating children's social inclusion and integration with their peers. The measures proposed below are intended to respond directly to issues of exclusion and disadvantage highlighted by children in the study.

Addressing exclusion within school

First, measures are needed to address the severe problems of exclusion within school that children have identified. School has rightly been a major target in the drive towards reducing child poverty, but these policies have been mainly about literacy standards, school exclusions and truancy. These are clearly very important areas, but what this study has shown us is that the social aspects of school life are especially important to children. There are several areas identified by children as causes for concern and there are measures that would act to address some of them directly.

School uniforms clearly play a valuable and protective role in children's lives; however, they are too costly and therefore do not protect children unless they can afford to buy the same as others. Many low-income families are forced to turn to the Social Fund for help with uniforms and this inevitably results in greater poverty from weekly deductions from benefits (CAB, 2001). Children and their families do not have a choice about school uniforms, and they are essential for social acceptance and social integration. Recent surveys have shown that the costs of providing a school uniform are prohibitive and place a great strain on low-income households (CAB, 2001; FWA, 2002). The Family Welfare Association found that the current cost of providing a school uniform was close to £100 for a child entering primary school and nearly £160 for one entering secondary school (FWA, 2002). However, while Estelle Morris, the current Education Secretary, has urged schools to cut the costs of their school uniform and to choose 'off the peg' items rather than expensive items available from only one specialist supplier, school heads are resistant to what they see as 'outrageous interference' from government (Woodward, 2002). Clearly, the initiative to support children from low-income families in school must come from government; the restoration of the uniform grant would directly address children's fears of difference, and relieve some of the pressure on already stretched family budgets. Furthermore, to avoid the stigma of applying to schools for uniform grants, local education authorities should administer the grants. This is particularly important in rural areas, where the experience of poverty is rarely a shared one and there is little privacy afforded children and parents in small local schools.

Increasing curricular demands have meant that trips away with the school are playing a growing role in enhancing children's experiences and knowledge prior to taking their exams. Social trips away with classmates are also an important part of school social life, and provide an opportunity to have fun while experiencing different surroundings and life-styles. Where children from low-income families had been able to go away with their schools, they had valued the experience immensely. Measures to guarantee free school trips and to ensure that an equitable allowance of school trips are available to all children is proposed. At present, schools are not legally allowed to charge parents for trips, only to request those parents make a voluntary contribution. However, as the interviews with parents in this study and in other studies (Middleton et al, 1994) have shown, parents are very uncertain about the effects of not paying the voluntary contribution, and can regard it as a form of coercion. Letters from schools can be misleading and in some cases appear to threaten parents with the withdrawal of the trip for all children if sufficient contributions are not forthcoming. Where schools do offer help it is often conditional. Children should be assured access to trips that are associated with the curriculum, and guaranteed the opportunity to share in at least one or more trips away each year that are purely for social reasons.

School exam projects were also areas for concern and it is proposed that schools are assisted to establish a fund for children and young people from low-income[5] families to draw on for materials required to fully participate in exam projects. A budget ceiling for all children when undertaking GCSE projects would also go some way towards ensuring greater parity between children in examinations.

It is also recommended that measures are taken to improve the qualification and delivery of free school meals. Nutritionally, free school meals have an important role to play in the health and development of children from low-income families[6]. However, it is also a shared social experience and one which children in the study were glad of. For many of these children free school meals were a valuable supplement, especially in families where food supplies at home were reduced and children were feeling hungry. However, for some children, particularly those living in rural areas, the experience of collecting the meal was so stigmatised as to make it undesirable. To resolve this a universal system of tokens or swipe cards[7] would ensure that all children collected their meals using the same currency, and that children receiving free school meals would be treated no differently to others.

Facilitating the involvement in social activities of children and young people from low-income families

Children's and young people's experiences outside of the school environment indicate a severe lack of opportunities to participate in shared activities with their friends and to develop and maintain wider social networks. Directly addressing these issues would mean facilitating both their involvement in activities and their ability to attend them.

At present the provision of concessionary help for children from low-income families is patchy and very dependent on the local council, or organising body of the activity. This situation needs to be greatly improved, and councils charged with ensuring that the activities they provide are accessible to children from low-income families. Access can be facilitated through the provision of free places and concessionary payments schemes. Some councils already operate a leisure passport scheme for low-income families and this could easily be extended as qualification for a much wider range of social activities. Other providers of children's activities and clubs also need to be encouraged and supported to provide places for children from low-income families, and to develop a deeper understanding of the kind of support children need to participate, which might include help with equipment and clothing where necessary. In this respect the new Children's Fund[8] could play a valuable role in supporting and encouraging local providers to be more aware of the needs of children from low-income families. There has been a considerable expansion in the provision of after-school care and clubs following the National Childcare Strategy; however, there is currently little provision that is targeted for those aged 10-14 (Kids Club Network, 2001). This is a neglected age group who find themselves on the margins of out-of-school services, often too young for youth clubs, but also too old for much of the present after-school provision (Day Care Trust, 2002). The provision of appropriate out-of-school services, that are affordable and attractive to young people, is an imperative if the needs of children from low-income families are to be met. Wherever possible children and young people should also be involved in identifying their needs and developing facilities in their neighbourhoods; when children and young people are meaningfully engaged in their local communities and neighbourhoods the results are significant and transformative (Henderson, 1995).

Young people's need for travel and leisure concessions is being addressed with the new ConneXions Card, targeted at all 16- to 19-year-olds in continuing education. However, the findings of this study would indicate that low-income children are in need of help with transport and leisure access at a much earlier age. Transport costs are a major barrier to children's access to friends and to participation in social events. This is particularly important for young people when they move between a half fare and an adult fare. To address these needs what is suggested is two forms of transport concession. The first would be one available to larger families on a low income and the other would be a travel card, for young people aged between 14 and 17, who are living in families in receipt of Income Support. This would facilitate not only greater social involvement, but also their involvement in part-time work, which many of these young people were seeking in order to provide their own resources.

Addressing the clothing needs of children and young people

The findings indicated the great difficulties children and young people were having meeting the clothing expectations of their social groups, and maintaining what they considered to be an acceptable social profile to ensure social inclusion with their peers. Directing help towards children's stated need for adequate clothes can be provided in two ways. First, the government should restore 'necessitous clothing grants' which used to be administered by local authorities. These were direct grants to low-income families to assist in the purchase of some new clothes for their children. In general, local authorities have an important role to fulfil in supporting children from low-income families, but all too often their anti-poverty strategies fail to take account of children's needs and rights (Cohen and Long, 1998). The system of delivery needs to be carefully thought out, to ensure that there is no element of stigma attached to receipt. This may entail looking at more radical forms of delivery, the use of catalogues for instance, that may serve to avoid the social discomfort of producing vouchers in local shops. This measure would provide essential material support for children and the opportunity to choose some new clothes, enabling them to 'fit in' more comfortably with their friends, and addressing their fears of difference.

Finally, it is important to reform the Social Fund. This is often the only option open to parents struggling to provide clothes and other necessities for their children. The provision of discretionary loans to the poorest people in our society is an iniquitous system, and should be replaced by a system of grants. This is particularly important where families are requesting help for their children. As we have seen, raising children on a restricted income places considerable strain on both parents and their children. Other research studies have shown that no matter how skilful or resourceful people are at managing on a low income, it is inevitable, given insufficient resources to meet needs, that people will be unable to manage (Millar and Ridge, 2001).

The way forward: listening to children and young people and responding to their needs

The issues raised by these children and young people from low-income families pose a challenge for society and for social policy. Whatever policies and provisions are chosen to respond to their concerns, they need to be child-centred in their concept, and the delivery should be adequate, non-stigmatising and based on needs identified by children and young people themselves. To do this entails a radical rethink about what is already available, such as free school meals, and the identification of good practice. Without addressing the issue of stigma, children will continue to lose out; therefore, careful thought about qualification and delivery of welfare is essential if we are to truly respond to the needs of children and young people.

The present government has shown an increasing inclination to engage with children and young people, particularly though the medium of the Children and Young People's Unit, and initiatives such as the government's proposals for a new strategy for all children and young people, set out in the consultation document *Tomorrow's future: Building a strategy for children and young people* (CYPU, 2001). The challenge is to ensure that children from low-income and disadvantaged families are included in meaningful consultations and participation, and that children's voices are listened to and acted on. Children's needs cannot be divorced from their families and communities that they are embedded in, and their well-being needs to be addressed across a wide range of initiatives (see Jack and Jordan, 1999; Smith, 1999).

As we have seen from this study, there is considerable value to be gained by engaging children and young people directly in the search for greater understanding and awareness of the experience of childhood poverty and social exclusion. As our knowledge and understanding about the methodological techniques required for a successful engagement with children develops, it is hoped that children's perspectives and meanings can be incorporated into many other areas of research and policy formulation. Child-centred research is not straightforward, however. It presents ethical and moral dilemmas, and often the findings threaten adult assumptions about children's lives. However, it is possible to bring a child's perspective to the analysis of childhood poverty and social exclusion. In doing so we gain a deeper insight into the realities of childhood poverty, one that is grounded in children's own experiences and meanings. The challenge ahead lies in responding to what we hear.

Notes

[1] It was not possible to separate an urban and rural sample in the quantitative study.

[2] Pupil Learning Credits (DfEE, 2001b) are intended to provide secondary schools with extra funding to enable disadvantaged children to participate in a whole range of school activities including school clubs and educational visits. These are to be piloted in a small number of schools, with a high percentage of pupils receiving free school meals.

[3] 'Strong ties' are the ties of family and neighbours, of kinship and care. 'Weak ties' are colleagues, acquaintances, and friends of friends, which 6 (1997) argues are particularly important as a medium of social advancement.

[4] Overall, around 1.59 million deductions were made from weekly Income Support payments in February 2000 from 1.16 million claimants of all client types (DSS, 2000b).

[5] Including children whose families are in receipt of Income Support/Jobseeker's Allowance, and those whose parents are low paid.

[6] The government introduced minimum nutritional standards for school meals in 2001 (Family Policy, 2000).

[7] The use of swipe cards is already in operation in some schools and deemed a success on more than one front. As well as reducing stigma for children receiving free school meals, they also serve to reduce bullying, as children do not carry money.

[8] The Children's Fund, worth £450 million over three years, supports two programmes. One is engaged in preventative work with 5- to 13-year-olds, and one in a £70 million network of 'local children's funds', administered by the voluntary sector and directed at local solutions for child poverty (HM Treasury, 2000b).

References

6, Perri (1997) *Escaping poverty*, London: Demos.

Abel-Smith, B. and Townsend, P. (1965) *The poor and the poorest*, London: G. Bell & Sons.

Abramovitch, R., Freedman, J. and Plinner, P. (1991) 'Children and money: getting an allowance credit versus cash, and knowledge of pricing', *Journal of Economic Psychology*, vol 12, pp 27-45.

Adelman, L. and Bradshaw, J. (1998) *Children in poverty in Britain: Analysis of the Family Resources Survey 1994/95*, York: Social Policy Research Unit, University of York.

Alderson, P. (1995) *Listening to children*, Ilford: Barnado's.

Alderson, P. (1999) *Civil rights in schools*, ESRC Research Briefing Paper No 1, Swindon: Economic and Social Research Council.

Allan, G. (1989) *Friendship: Developing a sociological perspective*, Hemel Hempstead: Harvester Wheatsheaf.

Alldred, P., David, M. and Edwards, R. (2000) *Children's understanding of parental involvement in education*, ESRC Research Briefing No 11, Swindon: Economic and Social Research Council.

Ambert, A.-M. (1995) 'Toward a theory of peer abuse', in A. Ambert (ed) *Sociological studies of children, vol 7*, Greenwich, CT: Jai Press, pp 177-205.

Anderson, I. and Quilgars, D. (1995) *Foyers for young people: Evaluation of a pilot initiative*, York: Centre for Housing Policy, University of York.

Archer, J. (1992) 'Childhood gender roles: social context and organisation', in H. McGurk (ed) *Childhood and social development*, Hove: Lawrence Earlbaum, pp 31-61.

Barber, M. (1996) *The learning game: Arguments for an educational revolution*, London: Victor Gollanz.

Bebbington, A. and Miles, J. (1989) 'The background of children who enter local authority care', *British Journal of Social Work*, vol 19, pp 349-68.

Beck, U. (1992) *Risk society: Towards a new modernity*, London: Sage Publications.

Becker, S., Aldridge, J. and Dearden, C. (1998) *Young carers and their families*, Oxford: Blackwell.

Beresford, P., Green, D., Lister, R. and Woodward, K. (1999) *Poverty first hand: Poor people speak for themselves*, London: Child Poverty Action Group.

Berghman, J. (1995) 'Social exclusion in Europe: policy context and analytical framework', in G. Room (ed) *Beyond the threshold: The measurement and analysis of social exclusion*, Bristol: The Policy Press, pp 10-28.

Berthoud, R., Lakey, J. and Mackay, S. (1993) *The economic problems of disabled people*, London: Policy Studies Institute.

Biehal, N., Clayden, J., Stein, M. and Wade, J. (1995) *Moving on*, London: HMSO.

Blair, T. (1999) 'Beveridge revisited: a welfare state for the 21st century', in R. Walker (ed) *Ending child poverty: Popular welfare for the 21st century?*, Bristol: The Policy Press, pp 7-18.

Blatchford, P. (1996) 'Pupils' views on school work and school from 7 to 16 years', *Research Papers in Education*, vol 11, pp 263-88.

Booth, C. (1902-03) *Life and labour of the people in London: First series: Poverty: Vol: East Central and South London*, London: Macmillan.

Boulton, M.J., Trueman, M., Chau, C., Whitehand, C. and Amatya, K. (1999) 'Concurrent and longitudinal links between friendship and peer victimisation: implications for befriending interventions', *Journal of Adolescence*, vol 22, pp 461-6.

Bowley, A.L. and Hogg, M. (1925) *Has poverty diminished?*, London: P.S. King.

Bradbury, B. and Jäntti, M. (1999) *Child poverty across industrialised nations*, Innocenti Occasional Papers, Economic and Social Policy Series No 71, Florence: UNICEF.

Bradbury, B. and Jäntti, M. (2001) 'Child poverty across the industrialised world: evidence from the Luxembourg Income Study', in K. Vleminckx and T.M. Smeeding (eds) *Child well-being, child poverty and child policy in modern nations: What do we know?*, Bristol: The Policy Press, pp 11-32.

Bradbury, B., Jenkins, S.P. and Micklewright, J. (2001) *The dynamics of poverty in industrialised countries*, Cambridge: Cambridge University Press.

Bradshaw, J. (1990) *Child poverty and deprivation in the UK*, London: National Children's Bureau.

Bradshaw, J. (1999) 'Child poverty in comparative perspective', *European Journal of Social Security*, vol 1, no 4, pp 383-406.

Bradshaw, J. (ed) (2001a) *Poverty: The outcomes for children*, London: Family Policy Studies Centre.

Bradshaw, J. (2001b) 'Child poverty under Labour', in G. Fimister (ed) *An end in sight*, London: Child Poverty Action Group, pp 9-27.

Bradshaw, J. and Barnes, H. (1999) 'How do nations monitor the well-being of their children', Paper to the Luxembourg Income Study Child Poverty Conference, York: Social Policy Research Unit, University of York, 30 September-2 October.

Bradshaw, J. and Holmes, H. (1989) *Living on the edge*, Tyneside and London: Child Poverty Action Group.

Brannen, J., Heptinstall, E. and Bhopal, K. (2000) *Connecting children care and family life in later childhood*, London: Routledge Falmer.

Brewer, M., Clark, T. and Goodman, A. (2002) *The government's child poverty target: How much progress has been made*, London: Institute for Fiscal Studies.

Brown, G. (2000) Speech by the Chancellor of the Exchequer to the CPAG Child Poverty Conference, London, 15 May.

Brynin, M. (1997) *Young people and smoking*, Working Paper 97-3, Colchester: Institute for Social and Economic Research, University of Essex.

Brynin, M. and Scott, J. (1996) *Young people, health and the family*, London: Health Education Authority.

Burgess, R. (1984) *In the field*, London: George Allen & Unwin.

Burnett, J. (1982) *Destiny obscure: Autobiographies of childhood, education and family from the 1820s to the 1920s*, London: Routledge.

Butler, I. and Williamson, H. (1994) *Children speak: Children, trauma and social work*, Harlow: Longman.

CAB (Citizens Advice Bureau) (2001) *Uniform failure: CAB clients' experiences of help with school uniform costs*, London: National Association of Citizens Advice Bureau.

Campaign for Learning (1998) *Attitudes to learning 98: MORI state of the nation survey: Summary report*, London: Campaign for Learning.

Carlen, P., Gleeson, D. and Wardhaugh, J. (1992) *Truancy: The politics of compulsory schooling*, Buckingham: Open University Press.

Carvel, J. (1999) 'Eight-year-olds to be given lessons on pocket money', *The Guardian*, 9 September.

ChildWise (2001) 'Insights on children's purchasing habits' (www.childwise.co.uk, 31 January 2002).

Christensen, P. and James, A. (2000) 'What are schools for? The temporal experience of learning', in L. Alanen and B. Mayall (eds) *Conceptualising child adult relationships*, London: Falmer Press, pp 70-85.

Christopher, K., England, P., McLanahan, S., Ross, K. and Smeeding, T. (2001) 'Gender inequality in poverty in affluent nations: the role of single motherhood and the state', in K. Vleminckx and T. Smeeding (eds) *Child well-being, child poverty and child policy in modern nations: What do we know?*, Bristol: The Policy Press, pp 199-219.

Clarke, L., Bradshaw, J. and Williams, J. (1999) 'Family diversity and poverty and the mental well-being of young people', Unpublished paper, London and York: London School of Hygiene and Tropical Medicine and University of York.

Cohen, R. and Long, G. (1998) 'Children and anti-poverty strategies', *Children & Society*, vol 12, pp 73-85.

Cohen, R., Coxall, J., Craig, G. and Sadiq-Sangster, A. (1992) *Hardship Britain*, London: Child Poverty Action Group.

Coles, B. (1995) *Youth and social policy: Youth citizenship and young careers*, London: UCL Press.

Cox, T. (ed) (2000) *Combating educational disadvantage: Meeting the needs of vulnerable children*, London: Falmer Press.

Cunningham, H. (1991) *Children of the poor*, Oxford: Basil Blackwell.

Cunningham, H. (1995) *Children and childhood in western society since 1500*, London: Longman.

CYPU (Children and Young People's Unit) (2001) *Tomorrow's future: Building a strategy for children and young people*, London: CYPU and The Stationery Office.

Daniel, P. and Ivatts, J. (1998) *Children and social policy*, Basingstoke: Macmillan.

Davin, A. (1996) *Growing up poor: Home, school and street in London 1870-1914*, London: Rivers Oram Press.

Davis, J. and Ridge, T. (1997) *Same scenery, different lifestyle: Rural children on a low income*, London: The Children's Society.

Davis, J. and Ridge, T. (1998) *Independent visitors: A study of need*, Midsomer Norton: The Children's Participation Project.

Day Care Trust (2002) *Older and bolder – A new approach to creating out of school services for 10 to 14 year olds*, London: Day Care Trust.

DfEE (Department of Education and Employment) (1997) *Excellence in schools*, Education White Paper, London: The Stationery Office.

DfEE (1999) *Education and labour market status of young people in England aged 16-18, 1992 to 1998, DfEE Statistical Bulletin, 11/99*, October, London: DfEE.

DfEE (2000) *ConneXions: The best start in life for every young person*, London: DfEE.

DfEE (2001a) *Transforming youth work: Developing youth work for young people*, London: DfEE.

DfEE (2001b) *Schools, building on success*, Cm 5050, London: The Stationery Office.

DHSS (Department of Health and Social Security) (1981) *Social security statistics 1981*, London: HMSO.

Ditch, J., Barnes, H., Bradshaw, J. and Kilkey, M. (1998) *A synthesis of national family policies*, European Observatory on National Family Policies, York: European Commission/Social Policy Research Unit, University of York.

DSS (Department of Social Security) (1994) *Social security statistics 1994*, London: HMSO.

DSS (1996) *Households Below Average Income: A statistical analysis 1979-1994/5*, London: The Stationery Office.

DSS (1998) *Cross benefit analysis: Population of working age on key benefits*, London: The Stationery Office.

DSS (1999a) *Opportunity for all: Tackling poverty and social exclusion*, Cm 4445, London: The Stationery Office.

DSS (1999b) *A new contract for welfare: Children's rights and parent's responsibilities*, July, London: DSS.

DSS (2000a) *Households Below Average Income: A statistical analysis 1994/5-1998/9*, Leeds: Corporate Document Services.

DSS (2000b) *Income Support quarterly statistics*, February, London: DSS.

DSS (2000c) *Public Service Agreement*, London: The Stationery Office.

Duffy, K. (1995) *Social exclusion and human dignity in Europe*, Background report for the Proposed Initiative by the Council of Europe, Steering Committee on Social Policy, Council of Europe.

Fraser, D. (ed) (1976) *The new Poor Law in the 19th century*, London: Macmillan.

DWP (Department for Work and Pensions) (2001) *Households Below Average Income: A statistical analysis 1999/2000*, Leeds: Corporate Document Services.

DWP (2002a) *Households Below Average Income: A statistical analysis 1994/95-2000/01*, Leeds: Corporate Document Services.

DWP (2002b) *Client group analysis: Quarterly bulletins on families with children on key benefits*, February, Newcastle-upon-Tyne: Analytical Services Directorate, DWP.

DWP (2002c) *Income Support quarterly statistical enquiry*, February, London: Analytical Services Division, DWP.

Ennew, J. (1994) 'Time for children or time for adults', in J. Qvortrup, M. Bardy, G. Sigritta and H. Wintersberger (eds) *Childhood matters: Social theory, practice and politics*, Aldershot: Avebury, pp 145-64.

Ennew, J. and Morrow, V. (1994) 'Out of the mouths of babes', in E. Verhellen and F. Spiesschaert (eds) *Children's rights: Monitoring issues*, Ghent: Myes and Breesch.

Ermisch, J., Francescanii, M. and Pevalin, D. (2001) *Outcomes for children of poverty*, DWP Research Report No 158, Leeds: Corporate Document Services.

Erwin, P. (1993) *Friendship and peer relations in children*, Chichester: Wiley.

Eurostat (1997) *Statistics in focus: Population and social conditions 1997*, Luxembourg: Eurostat.

Family Policy (2000) *Family policy*, Summer, London: Family Policy Studies Centre.

Feather, N.T. (1991) 'Variables relating to the allocation of pocket money to children: parental reasons and values', *British Journal of Social Psychology*, vol 30, pp 221-34.

Fine, G.A. and Sandstrom, K.L. (1988) *Knowing children: Participant observation with minors*, London: Sage Publications.

Furnham, A. (1989) 'Friendship and personal development', in R. Porter and S. Tomaselli (eds) *The dialectics of friendship*, London: Routledge, pp 92-110.

Furnham, A. (2001) 'Parental attitudes to pocket money/allowances for children', *Journal of Economic Psychology*, vol 22, no 3, pp 397-422.

FWA (Family Welfare Association) (2002) *Grants for school uniforms*, London: FWA.

Gilbert, B.B. (1966) *The evolution of National Insurance in Great Britain*, London: Michael Joseph.

Goldson, B. (1997) '"Childhood": an introduction to historical and theoretical analyses', in P. Scraton (ed) *Childhood in crisis*, London: UCL Press Ltd, pp 1-27.

Goode, J., Callender, C. and Lister, R. (1998) *Purse or wallet: Gender inequalities and income distribution within families on benefits*, London: Policy Studies Institute.

Gordon, D. and Heslop, P. (1999) 'Poverty and disabled children', in D. Dorling and S. Simpson (eds) *Statistics in society*, London: Arnold, pp 161-71.

Gordon, D., Adelman, L., Ashworth, K., Bradshaw, J., Levitas, J., Middleton, S., Pantazis, C., Patsios, D., Payne, S., Townsend, P. and Williams, J. (2000) *Poverty and social exclusion in Britain*, York: Joseph Rowntree Foundation.

Grant, L. (2000) 'Disabled people, poverty and debt: identity, strategy and policy', in J. Bradshaw and R. Sainsbury (eds) *Experiencing poverty*, Hampshire: Ashgate Publishing.

Greenfield, J., Jones, D., O'Brien, M., Rustin, M. and Sloan, D. (2000) *Childhood, urban space and citizenship: Child-sensitive urban regeneration*, Children 5-16 Research Briefing No 16, Swindon: Economic and Social Research Council.

Gregg, P. and Wadsworth, J. (1996) *It takes two: Employment polarisation in the OECD*, Discussion Paper No 304, London: Centre for Economic Performance, London School of Economics and Political Science.

Gregg, P., Harkness, S. and Machin, S. (1999) *Child development and family income*, York: Joseph Rowntree Foundation.

Guardian, The (2000) 'UK fails to provide path from school to work', 11 February.

Halsey, A.H. (1988) *British social trends since 1990: A guide to the changing social structure of Britain*, Basingstoke. Macmillan.

Hartup, W.W. (1992) 'Friendship and their developmental significance', in H. McGurk (ed) *Childhood and social development*, Hove: Lawrence Earlbaum, pp 175-206.

Haskey, J. (1998) 'One-parent families and their dependant children in Great Britain', in R. Ford and J. Millar (eds) *Private lives and public responses*, London: Policy Studies Institute, pp 22-41.

Hawker, D.S.J. and Boulton, M.J. (2000) 'Twenty years' research on peer victimisation and psychosocial maladjustment: a meta-analytic view of cross-sectional studies', *Journal of Child Psychiatry and Psychiatry*, vol 41, no 4, pp 441-55.

Henderson, P. (1995) *Children and communities*, London: Pluto Press.

Hendrick, H. (1994) *Child welfare: England 1872-1989*, London: Routledge.

Hendrick, H. (2003: forthcoming) *Child welfare in England: Historical dimensions, contemporary debate* (2nd edn), Bristol: The Policy Press.

Hendry, L., Shucksmith, M., Love, J. and Glendinning, A. (1993) *Young people's leisure and lifestyles*, London: Routledge.

Hill, M. (1992) 'Children's role in the domestic economy', *Journal of Consumer Studies and Home Economics*, vol 16, pp 35-50.

Hill, M. (1999) 'What's the problem? Who can help? The perspectives of children and young people on their well-being and on helping professionals', *Journal of Social Work Practice*, vol 13, no 2, pp 135-45.

Hill, M.S. and Jenkins, S.P. (1999) *Poverty among British children: Chronic or transitory*, ESRC Research Centre of Micro-Social Change Working Paper 92-23, Colchester: Institute for Social and Economic Research, University of Essex.

Hill, M.S., Laybourn, A. and Borland, M. (1996) 'Engaging with primary-aged children about their emotions and well-being: methodological considerations', *Children & Society*, vol 10, pp 129-44.

Hills, J. (1995) *Inquiry into income and wealth, Vol 2: Summary of evidence*, York: Joseph Rowntree Foundation.

Hills, J. (1998) *Income and wealth: The latest evidence*, York: Joseph Rowntree Foundation.

Hirsch, D. (1999) *Welfare beyond work*, York: Joseph Rowntree Foundation.

HM Treasury (1999) *Supporting children through the tax and benefit system*, London: HM Treasury.

HM Treasury (2000a) *Spending Review 2000: New public spending plans 2001-2004: Prudent for a purpose: Building opportunity and security for all*, London: The Stationery Office.

HM Treasury (2000b) *Budget, March 2000*, London: HM Treasury.

Hobbs, S. and McKechnie, J. (1997) *Child employment in Britain*, London: The Stationery Office.

Hobcraft, J. (1998) *Intergenerational and life-course transmission of social exclusion: Influences and childhood poverty, family disruption and contact with the police*, CASE Paper 15, London: Centre for the Analysis of Social Exclusion, London School of Economics and Political Science.

Hogan, D. and Gilligan, R. (1998) *Researching children's experiences: Qualitative approaches*, Dublin: The Children's Research Centre, Trinity College.

Holman, B. (2000) 'At the hard end, poverty lives', *New Statesman*, 15 May, pp 23-4.

Home Office (1999) *Supporting families*, London: Home Office.

Hood, S., Kelley, P. and Mayall, B. (1996) 'Children as research subjects: a risky enterprise', *Children & Society*, vol 10, pp 117-28.

Howard, M., Garnham, A., Finnister, G. and Veit-Wilson, J. (2001) *Poverty: The facts*, London: Child Poverty Action Group.

Howarth, C., Kenway, P., Palmer, G. and Street, C. (1998) *Monitoring poverty and social exclusion*, York: Joseph Rowntree Foundation.

Hutson, S. and Cheung, W.-Y. (1992) 'Saturday jobs: sixth formers in the labour market and the family', in C. Marsh and S. Arber (eds) *Families and households*, Basingstoke: Macmillan.

Jack, G. and Jordan, B. (1999) 'Social capital and child welfare', *Children & Society*, vol 13, no 4, pp 242-56.

James, A. (1993) *Childhood identities: Social relationships and the self in children's experiences*, Edinburgh: Edinburgh University Press.

James, A.L. and James, A. (2001) 'Tightening the net: children, community, and control', *British Journal of Sociology*, vol 52, no 2, June, pp 211-28.

James, A. and Prout, A. (1997) 'A new paradigm for the sociology of childhood? Provenance, promise and problems', in A. James and A. Prout (eds) (2nd edn) *Construction and reconstructing childhood*, London: Falmer, pp 7-33.

James, A., Jenks, C. and Prout, A. (1998) *Theorizing childhood*, Cambridge: Polity Press.

Jamieson, L. (2001) *Intimacy, personal relationships in modern society*, Cambridge: Polity Press.

Jenkins, S., Schluter, C. and Wagner, G. (2001) *Child poverty in Britain and Germany*, London: Anglo-German Foundation for the Study of Industrial Society.

Jensen, A.M. and Saporiti, A. (1992) *Do children count? A statistical compendium*, EUROSOCIAL Report 36/17, Vienna: European Centre for Social Welfare Policy and Research.

Jerrome, D. (1984) 'Good company: the sociological implications of friendship', *The Sociological Review*, vol 10, pp 117-28.

Jones, G. (1995) *Leaving home*, Milton Keynes: Open University Press.

Kay, J., Dr (1838) Document 4c, 'Report on pauper education', *Fourth Report by the Poor Law Commissioners*, Appendix, p 140.

Kempson, E. (1996) *Life on a low income*, York: Joseph Rowntree Foundation.

Kempson, E., Bryson, A. and Rowlingson, K. (1994) *Hard times*, London: Policy Studies Institute.

Keys, W. and Fernandes, C. (1993) *What do students think about school? Research into factors associated with positive and negative attitudes towards school and education*, Slough: National Foundation for Educational Research.

Kids Club Network (2001) *Teenage kicks: Childcare and out of school activities for 11-14 year olds: Good practice guide*, London: Kids Club Network.

Kiernan, K., Land, H. and Lewis, J. (1998) *Lone motherhood in twentieth century Britain*, Oxford: Clarendon Press.

Kumar, V. (1993) *Poverty and inequality in the UK: The effects on children*, London: National Children's Bureau.

Lansdown, G. (1994) 'Children's rights', in B. Mayall (ed) *Children's childhoods: Observed and experienced*, London: Falmer, pp 33-45.

Laslett, P. (1971) *The world we have lost*, London: Methuen & Co Ltd.

Lassarre, D. (1996) 'Consumer education in French families and schools', in P. Lunt and A. Furnham (eds) *Economic socialisation*, Cheltenham: Edward Elgar, pp 130-48.

Lavalette, M. (1994) *Child employment in the capitalist labour market*, Aldershot: Avebury.

Lawton, D. (1998) *Complex numbers: Families with more than one disabled child*, York: Social Policy Research Unit, University of York.

Leonard, M. (1998) 'Children's contribution to household income: a case study from Northern Ireland', in B. Pettitt (ed) *Children and work in the UK*, London: Child Poverty Action Group, pp 80-92.

Levitas, R. (1998) *The inclusive society: Social exclusion and New Labour*, Basingstoke: Macmillan.

Lewis, A., Webley, P. and Furnham, A. (1995) *The new economic mind*, London: Harvester Wheatsheaf.

Lewis, S.A. (2001) *Money in the contemporary family*, Nestle Family Monitor No 12, Croydon: Nestle UK Ltd.

Lister, R. (1990) *The exclusive society: Citizenship and the poor*, London: Child Poverty Action Group.

Lister, R. (2001) 'Doing good by stealth: the politics of poverty and inequality under New Labour', *New Economy*, June, vol 8, no 2, pp 65-70.

Lister, R., Goode, J. and Callender, C. (1999) 'Income distribution within families and the reform of social security', *Journal of Social Welfare and Family Law*, vol 21, no 3, pp 203-20.

Loader, I. (1996) *Youth, policing and democracy*, Basingstoke: Macmillan.

McCarthy, M. (1986) *Campaigning for the poor: CPAG and the politics of welfare*, London: Croom Helm.

Machin, S. (1999) 'Intergenerational transmissions of economic status', in P. Gregg (ed) *Jobs, wages and poverty: Patterns of persistence and mobility*, London: Centre for Economic Performance, London School of Economics and Political Science, pp 180-9.

McKechnie, J., Lindsay, S. and Hobbs, S. (1996) 'Child employment: a neglected topic?', *The Psychologist*, May, pp 219-22.

MacNicol, J. (1980) *The movement for family allowances, 1918-1945: A study in social policy development*, London: Heinemann.

Madge, N., Burtoin, S., Howell, S. and Hearn, B. (2000) *9 to 13: The forgotten years*, London: National Children's Bureau.

Mahon, A., Glendinning, C., Clarke, K. and Craig, G. (1996) 'Researching children: methods and ethics', *Children & Society*, vol 10, pp 145-54.

Marshall, H. (1964) 'The relation of giving children an allowance to children's knowledge and responsibility and to other practices of parents', *The Journal of Genetic Psychology*, vol 104, pp 35-51.

Marshall, H. and Magruder, L. (1960) 'Relations between parent, money, education practices and children's knowledge and use of money', *Child Development*, vol 31, pp 253-84.

Matthews, H. and Limb, M. (2000) *Exploring the 'Fourth environment': Young people's use of place and views on their environment*, ESRC Children 5-16 Research Briefing No 9, Swindon: Economic and Social Research Council.

Mauthner, M. (1997) 'Methodological aspects of collecting data from children: lessons from three research projects', *Children & Society*, vol 11, pp 16-28.

Micklewright, J. and Stewart, K. (2000a) 'Child well-being and social cohesion', *New Economy*, vol 7, no 1, March, pp 18-23.

Micklewright, J. and Stewart, K. (2000b) *Is child welfare converging in the European Union?*, Innocenti Occasional Papers, Economic and Social Policy series No 69, Florence: UNICEF Child Development Centre.

Middleton, S., Ashworth, K. and Braithwaite, I. (1997) *Small fortunes*, York: Joseph Rowntree Foundation.

Middleton, S., Ashworth, K. and Walker, R. (1994) *Family fortunes*, London: Child Poverty Action Group.

Miles, S. (1996) 'Use and consumption in the construction of identities', Paper presented at 'British youth research: the new agenda' conference, 26-28 January, Glasgow.

Millar, J. (1989) *Poverty and the lone-parent family*, Avebury: Gower.

Millar, J. (2000) *Report for the UK: Benefits for children: A four country study*, Ottawa, Canada: Caledon.

Millar, J. and Ridge, T. (2001) *Families, poverty, work and care: A review of the literature on lone parents and low-income couple families with children*, DWP Research Report No 153, Leeds: Corporate Document Services.

Millar, J. and Ridge, T. (2002) 'Parents, children, families and New Labour: developing family policy?', in M. Powell (ed) *Evaluating New Labour's welfare reforms*, Bristol: The Policy Press, pp 85-106.

Mingione, E. (1997) 'Enterprise and exclusion', in *The wealth and poverty of networks: Tackling social exclusion*, Demos Collection 12, London Demos.

Mizen, P., Bolton, A. and Pole, C. (1999) 'School age workers: the paid employment of children in Britain', *Work, Employment & Society*, vol 13, no 3, September, pp 423-38.

Mizen, P., Pole, C. and Bolton, A. (2001) 'Why be a school age worker?', in P. Mizen, C. Pole and A. Bolton (eds) *Hidden hands: International perspectives on children's work and labour*, London: Routledge Farmer, pp 37-54.

Modood, T., Berthoud, R., Lakey, J., Nazroo, J., Smith, P., Virdee, S. and Beishon, S. (1997) *Ethnic minorities in Britain*, London: Policy Studies Institute.

Moore, R. (2000) 'Material deprivation amongst ethnic minority and white children: the evidence of the Sample of Anonymised Records', in J. Bradshaw and R. Sainsbury (eds) *Experiencing poverty*, Hampshire: Ashgate Publishing.

Morrow, V. (1994) 'Responsible children? Aspects of children's work and employment outside school in contemporary UK', in B. Mayall (ed) *Children's childhoods: Observed and experienced*, London: Falmer.

Morrow, V. and Richards, M. (1996) 'The ethics of social research with children: an overview', *Children & Society*, vol 10, pp 90-105.

NAB (National Assistance Board) (1955) *Report of the National Assistance Board for the year ending 31st December 1954*, Cmd 9530, London: NAB, HMSO.

NAB (1964) *Report of the National Assistance Board for the year ending 31st December 1963*, Cmnd 2386, London: NAB, HMSO.

Nicaise, I. (ed) (2000) *The right to learn: Educational strategies for socially excluded youth in Europe*, Bristol: The Policy Press.

Oppenheim, C. and Harker, L. (1996) *Poverty: the facts*, London: Child Poverty Action Group.

Oxley, H., Dang, T.-T., Forster, M. and Pellizzari, M. (2001) 'Income inequalities and poverty among children and households with children in selected OECD countries', in K. Vleminckx and T.M. Smeeding (eds) *Child well-being, child poverty and child policy in modern nations: What do we know?*, Bristol: The Policy Press, pp 371-407.

Pahl, J. and Spencer, L. (1997) 'Friends and neighbours', *New Statesman*, vol 10, no 472, pp 36-7.

Pahl, R. (1998) 'Friendship: the glue of contemporary society?', in J. Franklin (ed) *The politics of risk society*, Cambridge: Polity Press, pp 99-119.

Pahl, R. (2000) *On friendship*, Cambridge: Polity Press.

Papadopoulos, T. (2000) *Welfare support for the unemployed: A comparative analysis of social policy responses to unemployment in twelve EU member states*, Aldershot: Ashgate.

Pellegrini, A.D., Bartini, M. and Brooks, F. (1999) 'School bullies, victims and aggressive victims: factors relating to group affiliation and victimisation in early adolescence', *Journal of Educational Psychology*, vol 91, pp 216-24.

Piachaud, D. and Sutherland, H. (2000) *How effective is the British government's attempt to reduce child poverty?*, CASE Paper 38, London: Centre for the Analysis of Social Exclusion, London School of Economics and Political Science.

Piachaud, D. and Sutherland, H. (2001) 'Child poverty: aims, achievements and prospects for the future', *New Economy*, June, pp 71-6.

Pinchbeck, I. and Hewitt, M. (1973) *Children in English society, Volume 11*, London: Routledge and Kegan Paul.

Platt, L. (2000) 'The experience of poverty: welfare dynamics among children of different ethnic groups', Unpublished thesis, Cambridge: Cambridge University.

Pollard, A. and Filer, A. (1996) *The social world of children's learning*, London: Cassell.

Poor Law Commissioners (1838) *Fourth Report by the Poor Law Commissioners*, London: Poor Law Commissioners.

Primarolo, D. (2001) 'Details announced of new tax credits to make work pay, support children and tackle poverty', 29 November (www.hm-treasury.gov.uk/newsroom_and_speeches/press/2001/press_132_01.cfm).

Prout, A. (2000) 'Children's participation: control and self-realisation in British late modernity', *Children & Society*, vol 14, pp 304-15.

Quilgars, D. (2001) 'Childhood accidents', in J. Bradshaw (ed) *Poverty: The outcomes for children*, London: Family Policies Study Centre, pp 56-65.

Qvortrup, J. (1985) 'Placing children in the division of labour', in P. Close and R. Collins (eds) *Family and economy in modern society*, Basingstoke: Macmillan.

Qvortrup, J. (1994) 'Childhood matters: an introduction', in J. Qvortrup, M. Bardy, G. Sigritta and H. Wintersberger (eds) *Childhood matters: Social theory, practice and politics*, Aldershot: Avebury, pp 1-23.

Qvortrup, J. (1997) 'A voice for children in statistical accounting: a plea for children's right to be heard', in A. James and A. Prout (eds) *Constructing and reconstructing childhood*, London: Falmer Press, pp 85-106.

Rathbone, E.F. (1924) *The disinherited family*, London: Allen & Unwin.

Ridge, T. (2000) 'A child-centred approach to childhood poverty and social exclusion', PhD Thesis, University of Bath.

Ridge, T. and Millar, J. (2000) 'Excluding children: autonomy, friendship and the experience of the care system', *Social Policy & Administration*, vol 34, no 2, pp 160-75.

Roaf, C. and Lloyd, C. (1995) *Multi-agency work with young people in difficulty?*, Oxford: Oxford Brookes University.

Roker, D. (1998) *Worth more than this: Young people growing up in family poverty*, London: The Children's Society.

Room, G. (1995) 'Poverty and social exclusion: the new European agenda for policy and research', in G. Room (ed) *Beyond the threshold: The measurement and analysis of social exclusion*, Bristol: The Policy Press, pp 1-9.

Rowlingson, K. and McKay, S. (2002) *Lone parent families, gender, class and the state*, Harlow: Prentice Hall.

Rowntree, B.S. (1901) *Poverty: A study of town life*, London: Macmillan.

Rowntree, B.S. (1941) *Poverty and progress*, London: Longmans, Green and Co.

Rubin, Z. (1980) *Children's friendships*, London: Fontana.

Ruddock, J., Chaplain, R. and Wallace, G. (1996) *School improvement: What can pupils tell us?*, London: David Fulton.

Ruxton, S. (2001) 'Towards a "children's policy" for the European Union', in P. Foley, J. Roache and S. Tucker (eds) *Children in society: Contemporary theory, policy and practice*, Basingstoke: Palgrave, pp 65-75.

Scott, J. (1994) *Poverty and wealth*, London: Longman.

Scott, J., Brynin, M. and Smith, R. (1995) 'Interviewing children in the British Household Panel Survey', in J.J. Hox, B.F. Van der Meulen, J.J.F. ter Laak and L.W.C. Travecchio (eds) *Advances in family research*, Den Haag: CIP-Gegevens Koninklijke Bibliotheek.

Scraton, P. (ed) (1997) *'Childhood' in 'crisis'?*, London: UCL Press.

SEU (Social Exclusion Unit) (1998a) *Bringing Britain together: A national strategy for neighbourhood renewal*, Cm 4045, London: The Stationery Office.

SEU (1998b) *Rough sleeping*, Cm 4008, London: The Stationery Office.

SEU (1998c) *Truancy and schools exclusion*, Cm 3957, London: The Stationery Office.

SEU (1999) *Teenage prregnancy*, Cm 4342, London: The Stationery Office.

Sharp, S. (1995) 'How much does bullying hurt? The effects of bullying on the personal well-being and educational progress of secondary aged students', *Educational and Child Psychology*, vol 12, pp 81-8.

Shropshire, J. and Middleton, S. (1999) *Small expectations: Learning to be poor?*, York: Joseph Rowntree Foundation.

Silva, E. and Smart, C. (1999) 'The "new" practices and politics of family life', in E. Silva and C. Smart (eds) *The 'new' family?*, London: Sage Publications, pp 1-12.

Smith, P.K. and Sharp, S. (eds) (1994) *School bullying: Insights and perspectives*, London: Routledge.

Smith, T. (1999) 'Neighbourhood and prevention strategies with children and families: what works', *Children & Society*, vol 13, no 4, pp 265-77.

Smith, T. and Noble, M. (1995) *Education divides: Poverty and schooling in the 1990s*, London: Child Poverty Action Group.

Sonuga-Barke, E. and Webley, P. (1993) *Children saving: A study in economic behaviour*, Hove: Lawrence Earlbaum Associates Ltd.

Sparkes, J. (1999) *Schools, education and social exclusion*, CASE Paper 29, London: Centre for the Analysis of Social Exclusion, London School of Economics and Political Science.

Thomas, N. and O'Kane, C. (1998) 'The ethics of participatory research with children', *Children & Society*, vol 12, pp 336-48.

Thompson, P., Lavery, M. and Curtis, J. (1990) *Short changed by disability*, London: Disability Income Group.

Thompson, T. (1981) *Edwardian childhoods*, London: Routledge.

Tout, H. (1938) *The standard of living in Bristol*, Bristol: Arrowsmith.

Vincent, D. (1981) *Bread, knowledge and freedom: A study of nineteenth century working class autobiography*, London: Europa Publications Ltd.

Vincent, D (1991) *Poor citizens: The state and the poor in twentieth-century Britain*, London: Longman.

Walker, A. (1990) 'The strategy of inequality: poverty and income distribution in Britain 1979-1989', in I. Taylor (ed) *The social effects of free market policies*, Hemel Hempstead: Harvester Wheatsheaf, pp 29-48.

Walker, A. and Walker, C. (eds) (1997) *Britain divided: The growth of social exclusion in the 1980s and 1990s*, London: Child Poverty Action Group.

Walker, R. (1995) 'Dynamics of poverty and social exclusion', in G. Room (ed) *Beyond the threshold: The measurement and analysis of social exclusion*, Bristol: The Policy Press, pp 102-28.

Walker, R. and Park, J. (1998) 'Unpicking poverty', in C. Oppenheim (ed) *An inclusive society: Strategies for tackling poverty*, London: Institute for Public Policy Research, pp 29-52.

Wall's (2001) *27th annual pocket money monitor 2001*, London: Wall's.

Ward, H. (1998) 'Poverty and family cohesion', Paper given to the Seebohm Rowntree Centenary Conference 18-20 March, York: University of York.

Webb, S. and Webb, B. (1929a, reprinted 1963) *English Poor Law history: Part I: The old Poor Law*, London: Frank Cass and Co Ltd.

Webb, S. and Webb, B. (1929b, reprinted 1963) *English Poor Law history: Part II: The last hundred years*, London: Frank Cass and Co Ltd.

White, B. (1996) 'Globalisation and the child labour problem', *Journal of International Development*, vol 8, no 6, pp 829-39.

Whitney, I. and Smith, P.K. (1993) 'A survey of the nature and extent of bullying in junior/middle school and secondary school', *Educational Research*, vol 35, no 1, pp 3-25.

Willis, P., Jones, S., Cannan, J. and Hurd, G. (1990) *Common culture: Symbolic work at play in the everyday cultures of the young*, Milton Keynes: Open University Press.

Woodward, W. (2002) 'Clamp put on cost of school uniforms', *The Guardian*, 28 February.

Wynn, M. (1968) *Fatherless families*, London: Michael Joseph.

Appendix: BHPYS Wave 7

The British Household Panel Youth Survey (BHPYS) provides a valuable opportunity to develop further the notion of child-centred data, as it utilises data generated by a large sample of children responding to issues relating to their own lives. However, it is a rarely used data set, perhaps reflecting the difficulties of using a data set which has a sample size of less than 800, but also reflecting in part our embedded culture of neither listening to nor valuing what children have to say.

The British Household Panel Survey (BHPS) is a complex data set with data recorded at the individual and household level. It is a household survey and also a panel study, so data is collected at different levels and individuals are tracked as they move in and out of households. The BHPYS contains data from children and young people who live in sample households and is also an ongoing panel study, with children moving into the panel at age 11 and then out into the adult survey at age 16. Chapter Six reports the findings from quantitative analysis of a cross-section of children and young people who responded to the Wave 7, 1997 survey.

Table A1 shows that there were 720 children and young people who responded to the youth questionnaire in the Wave 7 sample. Their ages ranged from 11 to 15, 53% of the sample were boys and 47% girls. To establish receipt of Income Support/Jobseeker's Allowance (IS/JSA), households were selected using variables indicating benefit type, benefit unit, and whether or not a household was currently in receipt of that benefit. Care was taken to ensure that only children living in households where their parents or main carers were in receipt of IS/JSA were coded as such[1]. Throughout the study, IS/JSA (benefit) children were compared to non-IS/JSA (non-benefit) children, and where significant

Table A1: Age and gender of BHPYS respondents (1997, Wave 7) (%)

Age[a]	Boys	Girls	Total
11	9	9	18
12	11	10	20
13	10	10	20
14	11	10	21
15	12	9	21
Total	53	47	100
Base (unweighted)	(379)	(341)	(720)

[a] For fieldwork reasons children who are 10 years old but turn 11 by 1 December 1997 are included as 11-year-olds, and 15-year-olds turning 16 by 1 December 1997 are excluded (and interviewed elsewhere as adults).

Source: Author's own analysis of BHYPS (1997, Wave 7).

differences emerged, further analysis was carried out. Preliminary exploration of the data indicated that age and gender were likely to be important factors and these variables were used throughout to try and unpick possible underlying explanations. For analysis purposes, children were coded into two age groups, pre-teenage (11-12 years) and teenage (13-15 years). Finally, multivariate analysis using variables derived from the main BHPS data was used to establish whether other factors were influencing the findings. These included classifications of household type, family type and whether the child was receiving money from paid work or not. Where these were significant, they are reported in the findings in Chapter Six.

Table A2 shows the main characteristics of children living in benefit and non-benefit households, and the variables used in the analysis. There were a balanced number of girls and boys, and slightly greater numbers of younger pre-teenage children in the benefit group than in the non-benefit group. Similar percentages of benefit and non-benefit children and young people were working. As might be expected there were substantially more lone-parent households in the benefit sample. However, these were not representative of children in the general benefit population as a whole. In the sample 55% of the benefit children lived in lone-parent families, whereas in the general public 81% of children living in families receiving IS or JSA were living in lone-parent families in 1997 (DSS, 1998).

All tables in Chapter Six are weighted using a BHPYS variable unless indicated otherwise. This provides an individual weight specific to the youth responses and weighted to reflect the true population on the basis of key characteristics such as age and gender. The weight is re-scaled by BHPS to ensure that overall the weighted total sample sizes are the same as for unweighted data. However, the total weighted sample size for the benefit sample is slightly raised from 112 to 114. Numbers of missing cases are indicated where they are more than 1% of the total sample.

Table A2: Characteristics of children (11-15 years) living in benefit and non-benefit households in BHPYS (1997, Wave 7) (%)

	Benefit	Non-benefit	All
Gender			
Boys	54	52	53
Girls	46	48	47
Base 100% (unweighted)	(112)	(608)	(720)
Ages			
Pre-teenage (11-12 years)	44	38	39
Teenage (13-15 years)	56	62	61
Base 100% (unweighted)	(112)	(608)	(720)
Household type			
Couple	42	80	81
Lone parent	55	11	18
Complex	3	1	1
Base 100% (unweighted)	(112)	(608)	(720)
Children's work status[a]			
Working	28	30	30
Not working	69	68	68
Did not respond	3	2	2
Base 100% (unweighted)	(112)	(608)	(720)

[a] 13 (2%) children and young people did not respond to this question.

Note

[1] With a complex data set including household and individual level data it is possible that households may appear to be in receipt of IS/JSA, but that this may relate to an older person, or a young single person living in the household.

Index

NOTE: page numbers in *italic type* refer to tables.